The *Creative* MARRIAGE

REVISED AND EXPANDED

The *Creative* MARRIAGE

THE ART OF KEEPING YOUR LOVE ALIVE

BESTSELLING AUTHORS

ED & LISA YOUNG

Dedication

WE DEDICATE THIS book to each other for staying devoted, true, and always committed to working on our marriage. We would also like to thank our parents for the invaluable gift of modeling commitment in their marriages. More than anything, we dedicate this book to the couples who will read it. Our prayer is that you will always put in the work to make your marriage creative and strong for your lasting journey together.

Contents

Introduction

SINCE FIRST WRITING this book, our lives have gone through many significant transitions. Lisa and I have been married for 40 years, and we have four adult children—EJ, Laurie, Landra, and LeeBeth (who is now in Heaven). We are also now grandparents! Through the revision of this book, we are again reminded of the relevancy of its content and how helpful it is as our lives continue to change through each stage of our marriage. While processing the passing of our eldest daughter, LeeBeth, we realized that you never stop parenting or working on your marriage. Don't wait until life's greatest challenges crash upon the shores of your relationship. Now is the time to prepare your marriage to thrive under any circumstances.

We won't ever be the same because of the pain we have had to process. But we will be better for it, because when God hands you a weight to carry, He gives it to you for a purpose. Because of God's supernatural presence, we've been able to walk on parallel tracks: one of deep sorrow and the other of outrageous, contagious joy. For the rest of our lives, we'll have a wound that is soft to the touch, but we know our pain is not in vain, and we trust God for the future.

Throughout our marriage and ministry, as we have maneuvered countless changes and stages, we have endeavored to make creativity a part of everything we do in life. Along the way, we have discovered that all of us are creative beings. We are creative because we are made in the image of our creative Creator. Thus, creativity should transcend every area of our lives, especially our marriages.

God invented marriage, and He designed it to thrive on creativity. Matthew 19:5 reveals God's plan from the very beginning: "For this reason a man will leave his father and mother and be united to his wife, and the two will become one flesh." God thought up marriage. It was His idea; He started the program. Your marriage is moving in one direction or another, and it takes creativity to keep that relationship moving in the right direction as you strive to meet your spouse's changing needs and live life united.

Jesus modeled marital creativity. The New Testament calls Christ the bridegroom and refers to the Church as the bride. God tells husbands to love their wives like Christ loved the Church. How much did Christ love the Church? Ephesians 5:25 says, "Christ loved the church and gave himself up for her."

God gave His life for us. We didn't deserve it—there is nothing you or I can do to merit what Jesus did for us—but with a self-sacrificing, holy, and pursuing love, Christ gave His life for His bride. Husbands, if you loved your wife like Christ loved the Church, you would set yourself up for a great marriage—something truly special. As you begin this book, ask God to give you the creative energy and drive you need to improve your marriage and take it to the next level. Then let Him work in your life as you make a commitment to building a creative marriage.

Our prayer is that this book will help you evaluate the creativity present in your marriage, make changes as needed, and build a safe union that reflects the presence of God in your life. We hope the truth found in this book is as helpful to your marriage as it has been to ours.

CHAPTER 1

A *Creative* Foundation

LAYING THE FOUNDATION
FOR A CREATIVE AND
LASTING MARRIAGE

1

I HAVE SAID it hundreds of times. At the conclusion of a wedding ceremony, I have looked into the starry eyes of the bride and groom and said, "I now pronounce you husband and wife, in the presence of God and these assembled witnesses." Then I add from the Bible, "What God has joined together, let no man separate." At this point, everything seems so perfect, so right. The man and the woman have just exchanged vows, rings, and kisses. The marriage is for keeps. Right?

Well, don't respond too quickly. Once you add a few kids, a few in-laws, a few financial problems, and the humdrum of life, marriage doesn't seem so certain anymore.

Some couples tell me, "Ed, we have a great marriage. We are more in love today than we were when we walked down the aisle. Marriage is great!"

Other couples shrug their shoulders and say, "Well, it's average. It's mediocre. I'm just doing time in this prison cell of predictability." They say, "Forever? How about foreclosure? My marriage is hanging by a thread. It's in the deep weeds."

Marriage matters to God; it is the most important earthly relationship we have. Sixty-one percent of all Americans will get married at least once in their lifetime, with nearly 50 percent of those marriages ending in divorce or separation. Many people who divorce will remarry within two years.

Even though marriages are failing in record numbers, millions still pursue it every single year. Marriage is the anchor of the family unit. It communicates volumes to our children. Good marriages can change our communities, our cities, our states, our nation, and even our world.

With so much at stake, it is important to go back to the very beginning of the marriage covenant and to the vows that hold it together.

THE VALUE OF THE VOWS

Do you remember everything you said on your wedding day? "To love, honor, and cherish, in sickness and in health, in prosperity and in adversity, leaving all others to keep only with each other as long as you both shall live." That's what I'm talking about.

"Wait a minute!" you exclaim. "I only said that once, and I was so terrified that I didn't even know what I was saying." None of us truly know the magnitude of what we're committing to on our wedding day. If we knew all that would be involved in our marriage relationship, most of us would probably be too scared to ever get married. But that's why those marriage vows are so critical. They provide a foundation of stability for your partner. They are a solemn promise that every one of us makes before God, a minister, our family, and our friends to keep the covenant of marriage through good times and bad.

Years ago, I accompanied Lisa to her twentieth high school reunion. As I walked into the hotel ballroom, lights were flashing, and the dance floor was packed. Videos of the glory days of high school were playing. People now 20 years older were still trying to "shake that groove thing" and "stay alive." It was also 20 times more entertaining to watch than in high school!

What was happening at this celebration? The reunion committee was attempting to bring the past into the present. They were trying to make events from 20 years ago current for today. And that is precisely what I want you to do with your vows. Take those promises you made before God and your witnesses during your wedding and pursue them passionately in the present.

A very close friend of mine was talking with me about marriage one day, and he said, "Ed, just after our honeymoon, my wife became desperately ill. She has been ill during our entire seventeen-year marriage. Nothing is normal about our marriage: intimacy is not normal, communication is not normal, sex is not normal." Then he looked at me and said, "When I recited those vows—when I said 'in sickness and in health'—I meant it. I meant it."

As my friend told me his story, I prayed silently, "God, let that be me." I hope you are willing to pray the same thing: "Let that be me." Remember to love, honor, and cherish, in sickness and in health, in prosperity and in adversity, forever.

This is not lightweight stuff. When you said your vows, you gave your word to God. You got into a covenant deal with Him. In the Old Testament, a covenant was an oath that required the spilling of an animal's blood. During the signing of this covenant, the Lord was called upon to witness the transaction. In other words, this was a significant decision.

Why not take your vows from the past and bring them into the present? Make them current. You wouldn't even think about walking out of the house in a new, trendy outfit accompanied by an old, outdated hairstyle. It would be irresponsible to let your insurance premium lapse. You wouldn't consider skipping your mortgage payment. You stay current with those things because they are priorities.

How much greater is the priority of marriage? Let me challenge you to stay current with your vows. I suggest you recite your vows to your spouse at least once a year. This would be a great way to celebrate your wedding anniversary each year. You don't have to repeat your vows word for word the way you did on your wedding day but put the same sentiment of those vows in your own words. Tell your spouse how much you love him or her. Let your spouse know you are serious about your commitment to love them and that your marriage is not based on flighty feelings. Remind them of your forever commitment, no matter what happens. Give them an assurance of your love, honor, and faithfulness. Let them know that nothing will come between the two of you as long as you live. Bring the promises of the past into the present, pursue them passionately, and continue to move those vows into the future.

I've taken the marriage vows and put them into current day vernacular: "I commit before God and you to creatively love, honor, and respect you; to be true to you in all situations for the rest of my life."

Why are these vows such a big deal? The vows begin, "I commit before God." We can talk about creativity until, as we say in Texas, the cows come home. We can talk about the value of the vows, but it all starts with God. We have to be on the same page

Marital math is two becoming one.

with Him. Our understanding of and appreciation for the marital commitment that comes from our vows flow from the commitment that God (through Christ) has already made to us. When we realize that God loves us unconditionally, we gain the endurance necessary to live a committed life for Christ and to have a dynamic and lasting marriage. Marital math is two becoming one.

For Christ-followers, that math takes on a whole new dimension because we have a special supernatural connection through our personal relationship with Christ. With this in place, Christ will give us the endurance and the ability to work, to create, and to keep up with our part of the vows.

When you are talking to your spouse and you have a communication breakdown, when you want to spin on your heels and walk out the door, suddenly your vows will echo in your mind. You may be able to write them even better than I did. Just don't forget that it all starts with God through your personal relationship with His Son, Jesus Christ.

> **We have a special supernatural connection through our personal relationship with Christ.**

When you get into a conflict and you feel the temperature rising, remember the value of the vows.

When one is in the mood for sex and the other is not, remember the value of the vows.

When you get to the end of a tough day and you're in a bad mood and want to lash out at your spouse, remember the value of your vows.

When parenting pressures begin to interfere with having a regular date night with your covenant partner, remember the value of the vows.

When sickness or financial trouble put a strain on your relationship, remember the value of the vows. Remember, remember, remember the value of the vows.

If I am going to remember the value of the vows—to love, honor, and respect—I must realize that living out these sacred promises takes a lot of work. A commitment to making your marriage successful requires you to roll up your sleeves and engage in grit-under-your-fingernails type of work. That's the next foundational aspect to building a creative marriage.

A TIRELESS MWE

One time I was boarding a flight to speak at a conference on the west coast. After I took my seat, I started watching the other passengers come aboard the plane. One man had a look on his face that clearly said he was having a bad day. He walked through First Class, looking enviously at the empty seats still there, and sat down in coach right across the aisle from me.

He was just spoiling for a fight. Shortly after the plane took off, he punched the seat of the guy in front of him and told him not to lean his chair back. Then this man craned his head to peer into the First Class cabin, where they had already started the beverage service.

Finally, when the flight attendant walked by, he said, "Excuse me, honey. I noticed some empty seats in First Class. Are there any available?"

She smiled sweetly and replied, "There are some empty seats, but there are none available for you."

The man sat there stewing. After a minute he took out his wallet and looked through some cards. The same flight attendant walked back, and he said to her, "Miss, I have this travel agent card, and I wondered if you would put me up in First Class."

She smiled again, said "No," and kept walking.

What was happening here? This man was trying to get into First Class, but he hadn't paid the price.

The same is true in marriage. If you want to have a "First Class" marriage, you have to pay the price. The price tag is lots of hard work, but the reward is well worth it.

Great marriages maintain a tireless MWE—Marital Work Ethic. The sad thing is, we are all dialed into the desire for instant gratification that permeates our culture. If it is not quick, easy, express, overnight, or disposable, we don't want anything to do with it. We think if it takes a lot of work and involves a lot of time, it can't be that gratifying.

Then one day, we get married and discover that marriage takes work, negotiation, sweat, toil, pain, and sacrifice, and that it is for keeps. Our disposable culture clashes with the permanency of the marriage relationship. No wonder so many marriages today end in divorce.

Ask God to develop within your spirit a tireless Marital Work Ethic. Marriage takes work, and carrying out that work in positive and consistent ways through decades of change takes creativity. Therefore, we desperately need marital creativity.

We fall in love when another person meets our emotional needs. Because the demands of those needs change over time, meeting them on a daily basis takes creativity and work. My needs at 21 were different from my needs at 31, and they are different from my needs now.

Love begins to wane when a spouse says they don't want to meet those emotional needs anymore. And people can decide not to meet those needs for a number of reasons. Some will say, "Forget the Marital Work Ethic. I have other things begging for my attention." Some just keep on doing what they have always done—the same thing, the same way—expecting different results. Isn't that the definition of insanity?

You have to understand that doing things the same old way just won't work, because our emotional needs are moving targets.

These emotional needs are met when you study your spouse. You have to really understand them if you want to meet their needs. This doesn't come easily, but it is well worth the effort. Love flourishes in a marriage when both partners are working to meet the needs of the other.

You may be reading this and thinking, *Okay, Ed, it's easy for you to write about marriage. You've been married for 40-plus years, and you have a great marriage. You're a pastor, so you have it all together. You have no idea what my marriage is like.*

Lisa and I do have a great marriage. I love Lisa more today than I did four decades ago. But I go through the same challenges, the same conflicts, and the same temptations that you do. I am a human being, and you are a human being. We're in this thing together.

Marriage has taken a lot of work for Lisa and me, but the work is worth it. I find that couples hit a relational sticking point and don't work on the personal junk that is at the root of their problems. They simply throw in the towel, abandon their vows, and opt for a divorce. Instead of looking for creative solutions to their marital problems, they take the same junk into the next marriage and the next marriage and the next marriage.

> Love flourishes in a marriage when both when both partners are working to meet the needs of the other.

Situations like this get ridiculous quickly. Deal with the junk now. Work on it and keep working on it for as long as it takes. Make a commitment before God to keep creativity in your marriage for the long haul: "God, this deal is for keeps. I am going to make creativity and innovation permanent features in my marriage."

God is doing great things, and He wants to do even greater things in every marriage. My marriage needs improvement. Your marriage needs improvement. So let's develop and live out the value of our vows as we commit to a Marital Work Ethic. Marriage is for keeps, and infusing it with creativity will change the course of our lives.

One summer, I took my family to California on a vacation. I was driving late one night, around 11 pm, in a Suburban packed with our four kids plus some friends we had with us. I was talking (because I talk a lot), and Lisa was giving me directions (because I am directionally challenged). Suddenly, in my rear-view mirror, I saw a sight that causes some people to say words under their breath that I should not utter as a pastor.

"Oh, Lisa, I'm being pulled over." I slowed down and pulled off the road. This was just after I had led the youth beach retreats at our church, where several of the other pastors and I had dyed our hair platinum blonde. And it was still blonde—horribly blonde.

The police officer came over to the window, leaned in, and said, "Sir, you were swerving a little bit. What have you been up to tonight?"

I replied, "Just finished grabbing dinner with my family and some friends. I'm a pastor in the Dallas/Fort Worth area."

He looked at me—specifically at the platinum blonde hair—and said, "Right. I need to see your license, sir." I started rummaging around trying to find my license while making light conversation with him.

The officer wasn't amused. He looked at my driver's license, then at the car, and said, "Well, there are a lot of dangerous drivers on this stretch. I can see you're on your vacation with your family. Just keep your car within the lines, okay?"

In a real sense, God is patrolling the highways of our lives, isn't He? A lot of marriages are swerving, going this and that direction. And like that highway patrolman, God will pull us over, check our marriages out, and send us on our way. He'll say, "Stay between the lines. Stay within My parameters, My guardrails, and My ground rules for a successful marriage."

You can have a great marriage. God wants you to have one. He is your biggest cheerleader in marriage. But first, you must be willing to say, "I am ready to do whatever it takes to have a successful relationship with my spouse. I want to do it God's way." Having a great marriage begins with you and God.

> You must be willing to say... "I am ready to do whatever it takes to have a successful relationship with my spouse. I want to do it God's way."

When you read a book about marriage, I know how tempting it is to think about your spouse's issues instead of your own. It will be tempting to think at certain points in this book, *Ed, thank you for hitting him between the eyes. He needs that so much. Get him, Ed. Tear him from limb to limb.* Or *She's been doing that to me for the last three years! Thank you so much for saying that, Ed. I'm going to leave the book open right here on the coffee table, and maybe she'll get the idea.*

Let's not do that. I don't need to think about Lisa, and she doesn't need to think about me. We need to think about our own need for change. Many of us are so obsessed with what our spouse is doing, not doing, or should be doing that we forget to think about what we need to change in our own lives. Allow God to work in your heart and mind to help you discover how to make your marriage more vibrant, more alive, and more creative than ever before.

The Basics of a *Creative* Foundation

- Make sure God is the center of your marriage. God created the institution of marriage, and He created you. Know that He is cheering you on as you work to improve your relationship with Him and your spouse.

- Think about the creative potential you have been given by your creative God. Just as you use this creativity in the workplace, apply these gifts to your marriage.

- Ask God to strengthen your resolve as you recommit yourself to your vows. Pursue the vows you made in the past with passion in the present.

- Charge up your MWE (Marital Work Ethic). Roll up your sleeves and invest in the most important relationship you will ever have outside of your relationship with Christ.

CHAPTER 2

Creative Communication

BUILDING AND BENEFITING YOUR SPOUSE THROUGH POSITIVE COMMUNICATION

2

TAKE A COUPLE minutes and let the following phrases sink in.

- Ephesians 4:29: "Do not let any unwholesome talk come out of your mouths, but only what is helpful for building others up according to their needs, that it may benefit those who listen."
- Proverbs 25:11: "A word fitly spoken is like apples of gold in a setting of silver" (ESV).
- James 1:19: "Everyone should be quick to listen, slow to speak."

If you didn't recognize them, I just quoted several verses from the Bible, each centering on the topic of communication. The Bible is a treatise on speaking and listening.

Husbands and wives, think back for a second to when you were dating, when everything—especially communication—was just flowing. It seemed so easy and effortless, didn't it? Do you remember the hours upon hours of phone conversations, the long walks, and the two of you talking in restaurants until closing time?

The moment the pastor pronounced you husband and wife, the moment he signed the marriage license, you expected communication to deepen, didn't you? You still expected those romantic talks. You still expected the long walks. You still expected to be closing down restaurants.

But something changed, something you can't quite put your finger on. Conversation became a little tired, a little predictable, and a little stale. Maybe you moved from long walks to short errands. Maybe you stopped closing down restaurants and started using drive-through windows.

Instead of exchanging long, romantic phone conversations, you began exchanging text messages. Your talks may have turned from dreams, desires, plans, and promises to one- and two-word sound bites. Maybe, just maybe, your communication (your talking and listening skills) aren't quite what they used to be.

What separates the great marriages from the not-so-great ones is obvious. Great marriages are made up of men and women who tenaciously tackle the task of great communication. And there are three necessary ingredients for effective communication. All you need is an active mind, a couple of ears, and a mouth. The key is to engage all these powerful resources to interact with your spouse. You have the power to be a great communicator, but it takes work and persistence.

Great marriages don't "just happen." These marriages have dedicated husbands and wives who work at their marriages tirelessly, especially in the area of communication. It all goes back to the tireless Marital Work Ethic (MWE) we talked about earlier. Both partners must make a commitment to work together creatively at having regular, strategic communication.

Struggling marriages don't "just happen" either. Troubled relationships most often are a result of neglect and a poor MWE. The marriage may have started out with a bang and thrived for several years, but over time marital drift came on the scene. And instead of working through the communication issues in marriage (yes, we all have them), these couples threw their hands up in surrender, saying, "Well, that's just the way it is. There's nothing we can do about it." You have to fight for your marriage. You need to fight to stay close to your spouse, to communicate even when it's painful, and to use all your creative resources to blast through barriers when your marriage is bland, and your problems seem insurmountable.

No area in marriage needs innovative action, creativity, and a tireless MWE like communication. It influences every other aspect of our relationship. As communication goes, so conflict resolution will go. As communication goes, so sex will go. As communication goes, so intimacy and romance will go. The list is endless.

We have a couple of options when it comes to communication. These options are revealed in Ephesians 4:29. It starts, "Do not let any unwholesome talk come out of your mouths." Our first option is unwholesome talk. But what exactly does "unwholesome" mean?

On a hot Texas day in June, I took Landra, one of my then five-year-old twins, fishing. We had a wonderful time catching perch at a little pond near our house.

> As communication goes, so conflict resolution will go. As communication goes, so sex will go. As communication goes, so intimacy and romance will go.

Landra, like most children, was emotionally attached to each fish we caught and wanted to keep them all. Now, my general rule is to return the fish I catch, but I told Landra she could keep one to show her mother.

I didn't realize, however, how mischievous Landra could be. While she held one fish in her hand—the one I told her she could keep—she had also hidden another fish in the tackle box.

We drove home, and she showed the fish to everyone. Lisa, as always, was a very proud and affirming mom. We even took a picture of the six-inch fish. After that "picture perfect moment," I unloaded the truck and put the tackle box in the garage.

Push the clock forward several days and add some triple-degree Texas heat. Lisa looked at me one afternoon and said, "Honey, something smells awful in our garage. It smells like a dead animal."

Since our house backs up to some woods, it was entirely possible that a small forest creature had crawled into the garage, among all the bikes and roller blades, to breathe its last breath.

I'm not known for great eyesight, but I do have a great sense of smell, so I was on top of this one. "No problem, Lisa," I declared. "I will sniff it out."

I walked into the garage and put my powerful sniffer to work. As I neared the source, I thought I detected the smell of a rotten fish. But there was no way a fish could have found its way into our garage. Right? WRONG! My nose led me to the corner where I keep my fishing supplies. The smell was coming from—you guessed it— the tackle box.

I opened the tackle box, and the stench nearly knocked me out. It was horrific! With newfound freedom, the fumes seeped under the door and crept into the house. Needless to say, Lisa was not happy.

As I was studying Ephesians 4:29, I looked up the original meaning for the word "unwholesome." It literally means spoiled fish. Husbands and wives, we can spoil our spouse's spirit with our words and with our failure to really listen to them.

Have you ever been around a couple where you could just smell the rotten fish? You can tell they have rotting perch in their lives because of the unwholesome talk that rolls off their tongues. They tear apart self-esteem, using phrases like "You never," "You always," or "Do you realize how fortunate you are to be married to me?" It is unwholesome talk—spoiled fish.

That is one communication option that we have, but I hope you'll agree that it's not our best option. Spouses, we wield such power with our words because of the octane behind them. And so many times, we don't realize the damage they can do. Don't spoil your spouse's spirit. Don't put dead fish in your spouse's tackle box.

Thankfully, there is another option. Look again at Ephesians 4:29: "Do not let any unwholesome talk come out of your mouths, but only what is helpful for building others up according to their needs, that it may benefit those who listen."

We can either spoil our spouse's spirit, or we can build it up and benefit them through positive communication. I should say to Lisa only what is helpful for building her up, like "I admire you for that," "You do that so well," and "Even if no one else notices what you bring to the table, I do, and I thank you for it."

> **No one else has the power to restore you with words like your spouse.**

There is nothing like being energized by your spouse. A compliment from a co-worker or a friend is nice, but no one else has the power to restore you with words like your spouse.

I like the next part of the verse where it talks about building one another up "according to their needs." People who are great communicators work at it. They discern the situation and learn how to respond. They have appropriate replies, words, looks, and nods for the situation.

The verse ends, "that it may benefit those who listen." Some translations say it this way: "that it may give grace to those who hear" (ESV). In other words, my voice box can be a vehicle for God to bless others by giving His grace to the people I talk to.

When I communicate words of love to Lisa, God can use my vocal cords to communicate His love for her, His understanding of her, His encouragement to her, and His compassion for her.

A COMMUNICATION BREAKTHROUGH

One question begs to be answered: *How?* "Sure, Ed," you may say, "I don't want to spoil my spouse's spirit. I know that I have stepped over the line; I have thrown some spoiled perch his or her way, but I want to change. How do I do it?"

Well, there are several things we can do to ramp up our learning curve and several practical steps we can take to build and benefit our spouse. These steps are essential elements in the art of keeping love alive in marriage.

But before I go through these steps, there is one caveat. This is not for the faint of heart. What I'm talking about is difficult. It is tough. It is work. But it's worth it. I communicate for a living, and I still have a long way to go in this department. If you don't believe me, ask Lisa.

I want to share with you in an open, honest, and authentic way some struggles we have gone through and some good things we have done to help our communication. I think Lisa and I have great communication. Can we improve? Yes. I am looking forward to the 20 percent improvement rate after writing this book, and so is Lisa.

TAKE A TECH BREAK

Remember that Kit Kat® candy bar commercial? "Gimme a break, gimme a break, break me off a piece of that Kit Kat bar." What about one of America's most popular fast-food restaurants, McDonald's? "You deserve a break today!" I'm not a big junk food guy, but you have to love the creativity of these ad campaigns. I remember those jingles vividly, even though they came out years ago. Did you notice that both ads targeted the word "break?" I think they picked up on something very important. We are all going at a mile-a-minute pace. We are stressed. We pack on as much as we can—and then we add even more. How about your marriage? Ever thought of taking a break to build your relationship?

I'm talking about giving your marriage a technology break. Have you noticed how technology can both help and hurt you at the same time? I love technology, but I've found that it is an easy way for Lisa and me to get side-tracked from our relationship. For these technology breaks to be effective, they must be intentional and strategic. Don't just wait for eyestrain or carpel tunnel syndrome to set in before taking time off from the distractions of technology.

It all comes down to priorities, doesn't it? You need to set priorities and plan times off when you are giving full attention to your spouse. Most of us are so wired in, hooked up, and freaked out over technology that we allow the digital world to creep in and steal precious moments from our marital relationship.

Lisa and I have a regular date night (usually once a week but at least twice a month). One night, while driving us to our date destination, I had my phone glued to my ear. I was talking about work and dealing with church business. I had lots of big, important stuff that I just had to talk about at that particular time. After all, I am the senior pastor, and I have to be available 24/7 ... yada, yada, yada. The rationalization can go on and on.

After about 45 minutes of conversation, I could tell I had messed up. I had allowed technology to take away some precious moments with my wife. As I look back on that date night, I have no idea what business I was talking about on my phone. I really have no clue. But I do know I missed those precious moments of communication because I had allowed technology to eat away at our time together.

Technology is paradoxical, isn't it? We have all these things that enhance communication: e-mail, voicemail, texting, etc. The list is limitless. Yet these very things usually end up hurting communication with the people we care about the most. These wonderful devices have all been the driving force in our modern-day business world, but their very pervasiveness in our daily lives can jam the airwaves of honest, open, and regular marital communication.

Here is what Lisa and I have done. Several times a week, we take what I call a "phone fast." We both put our phones on "do not disturb" and resist the urge to check them.

I discovered something awhile back: I own my phones. My phones don't own me. I am not obliged to answer the phone when I don't want to. When the kids were younger, we would go through a phone fast for two to three hours and spend time with just our family.

Lisa and I also spend time talking—just the two of us. We have learned that you must push the electronic devices away to get that time in. Ask yourself, *Am I too locked in? Could technology be taking away from my communication with my spouse?*

PLAY IN THE RIGHT ZONE

The next suggestion is something I call respecting your spouse's time zone. If I am going to build and benefit my spouse and become a great communicator, then I must respect their time zone. Have you noticed that opposites attract? Sometimes a night owl will marry a morning person.

Let's say, for example, that the husband is a "PM person," and the wife is an "AM person." Sometimes the husband will try to coerce and even shame his morning spouse into flying into his time zone: "Come to my time zone. That is when I am alert. That is when I am hitting on all cylinders. You'll love it, too. Come over here with me." Give it up. It's just not going to work, and it's also not fair to your spouse.

I am naturally a night owl, and Lisa is naturally a morning person. We have compromised by establishing a joint time zone. I go to bed earlier than I normally would, and she goes to bed later than she normally would. We now have *our* time zone, when we are alert, geared up, and ready to communicate. When the two of you discover your time zone sweet spot, you'll find that your ability to communicate will be at its peak. I encourage you to do some time zone work.

The writer of the book of Proverbs hit this one right on the head: "Timely advice [communication at the right time] is lovely, like golden apples in a silver basket" (Proverbs 25:11 NLT). Hey, wives, how would you like to get jewelry from your husband every single day? Well, this verse says you can. He can give you verbal jewelry if he communicates at the right time in your time zone.

OBSERVE SPEED-LIMIT SIGNS

Another way to build and benefit your spouse is to observe speed-limit signs. In our helter-skelter society, we have to find ways that will allow us to slow down and exit Busy Boulevard. Or for the international traveler, lose the Autobahn mentality. Some of us need to recognize our own speed limits, step on the brakes, and take the off-ramp to a slower and more meaningful life. No matter how much we want to deny it, we all have limits. We are not machines, and we need to stop acting like we are.

Most of us are over-challenged, over-committed, and over-stimulated. We are shopping and soccering and recreating our way into oblivion. We are traveling at such high speeds that we will end up hydroplaning over the most important earthly relationship in the world—our relationship with our spouse.

When we are driving on Busy Boulevard, the conversation usually goes like this:

"How was your day?"
"Fine. What's for dinner?"
"I don't know."
"What time is soccer practice?"
"Six. I love you."
"I love you, too."

We get into that fast lane, and we push the major things—those heartfelt conversations and those spiritual dialogues—to the shoulder of the road. Then one day, during our annual moments of introspection, we look in the rear-view mirror, see wreck after wreck in our marriage, and wonder what happened. What happened is that we continued to live life on Busy Boulevard and zoomed right past what should have mattered most to us.

> We are traveling at such high speeds that we will end up hydroplaning over the most important earthly relationship in the world—our relationship with our spouse.

Every time I speak publicly about setting priorities during one of my messages at church, people run up to me and thank me. They tell me how inspiring it is for a pastor to talk about eliminating activities to spend more time with their spouse and kids. And then they state their intentions to change. Most of these people, however, are right back on Busy Boulevard after a few weeks. Talk is great, but we must follow up our intentions with actions if we are truly going to change. We have to fight. We have to be tenacious about our time. If we want great communication, then we must make a daily resolve to observe our speed limits.

PURSUE RECREATIONAL COMPANIONSHIP

Marital communication has the opportunity to bloom and blossom when, as partners and friends, we discover and participate in a mutually enjoyable activity. I'm not talking about sex here. (Sorry to disappoint you, guys, but at least I got your attention!) Recreation is another vital ingredient for a dynamic marriage. We have to discover a mutually desirable activity where the husband and wife can just play together.

Some of you might say, "Well, we just don't have anything in common anymore. We just never talk." Have you taken the time and effort to find something fun to do together on a regular basis? Have you tried exercising together or taking an art class together? It could be skiing. It could be kickboxing. It could be power walking or jogging.

Lisa and I exercise a lot together. I can run a lot faster than Lisa and can smoke her in a race, but I don't. Do you know why? I have discovered that when we run side-by-side, we can actually communicate and enjoy each other's company. That's hard to do that when you are a quarter mile up the road! I would rather jog slower and communicate more than jog faster and communicate less.

Our conversation flourishes during these casual and recreational times together. In fact, we often talk more freely and comfortably while we jog than when we intentionally sit down and try to force the same kind of meaningful conversation.

Let me also add that watching TV or movies together is not the kind of recreational activity I am referring to in this section. Television tends to stifle meaningful conversation rather than foster it. I encourage you to find an activity that forces both of you to get off the couch and fosters meaningful communication. Don't get me wrong; I enjoy watching television and going to the movies from time to time. Lisa and I will watch movies for a quick escape from reality, but we know they aren't a substitute for marital communication. After watching a movie, we'll usually end up drinking coffee and talking about the movie and the events surrounding our lives. We've found that the combination of a movie and a conversation over a cup of coffee is a wonderful way to unwind from a busy week and build up our marriage at the same time.

Recently, we kayaked across a nearby lake. You would not believe how many good conversations came from that simple activity. Spending this recreational time together provides a non-threatening outlet for catching up with each other's lives, thinking about important issues, and really listening to each other.

Wives, do you know what one of your husband's biggest needs happens to be? You may not believe it, but the answer is recreational companionship. Now, I am not saying that you should spend three days in a deer blind or move to a houseboat on the lake. But I am encouraging you to find something that you enjoy doing together.

DO THE MATH

We can build and benefit our spouse in another way. I must warn you, though: this one is really going to hit close to home. This is what I call the "216 Principle."

Lisa and I have four children, and we love them dearly. They are gifts from God, and we would give our lives for them. When our children were young, I did the math and discovered that we were only going to have each child about 216 months from birth until 18 years. After that, they were out of the house and on their own—or at least that was the goal.

Well, 216 months pales in comparison to a lifetime. I am not married to my children. I am married to Lisa. And my marriage to her is more important than my relationship with my kids. A lot of us have that mixed up and out of focus.

Children let their needs be known rapidly. "I skinned my knee." "I got cut from the basketball team." These are 9-1-1 situations. We must help them, love them, pat them on the back, and counsel them. But parents run into trouble when they begin to revolve everything in the home around their children (see Chapter 6 on the spouse-centric home).

> **I am not married to my children. I am married to Lisa. And my marriage to her is more important than my relationship with my kids.**

Couples who do this neglect their marriage, their communication, their intimacy, and their romance. And one day they wake up after 216 months and say to their spouse, "Who in the world are you?" That's why I know it is so important for Lisa and me to make the time at least twice a month to go out on a date together, just the two of us.

"Well, Ed, you don't understand my schedule. My children have all these athletic events and school activities." Hey, if that is your life, it is probably too busy. Exit Busy Boulevard. Lose the Autobahn mentality. I am all for extra-curricular activities, but parents, don't overdose on them. You have to keep your marriage as the top priority. If you don't, you will eventually look in that rear view mirror and wonder what went wrong.

I have talked to couples who have infants and children in preschool. They say they would love to go out, but their children cry when they leave, and they don't like babysitters. I understand where they are coming from. I remember how hard it was to leave our infant and preschool children in the hands of a babysitter. Later in life when our children grew older, they would still give Lisa and me a hard time about leaving for our date night. But it taught them that the husband-wife relationship is the highest priority in the family. It taught them that Mommy and Daddy love to spend time together.

Parents, let me remind you that although the date night is intended to strengthen us, it also serves to strengthen our children It teaches them that even though Mommy and Daddy leave, they will come back happier and stronger.

It is much better to allow your preschooler or infant to cry a little bit than for you to spend a lifetime of remorse because you neglected your relationship with your spouse. So put into practice the 216 Principle.

After the twins were a month old, our pediatrician asked if we had gone out on a date yet. She asked if we had spent time together, just the two of us. This was great counsel, and we continue to follow it to this day.

People often ask Lisa and me about the secret to our great marriage. The primary secret to a great marriage is the foundation we have in Christ. But after that, I believe that one of the key ingredients is the time we spend together, specifically the date night. We have to fight for it, but it is worth it. If we invest wisely in communication and recreation with our spouse, we will be happy and ready for the empty nest at the end of those 216 months.

THE SWEET SIXTEEN

Another way to benefit our marriages and have great communication is to have an R.C. I used to work with a gentleman about two decades ago by the name of R.C. Smith. R.C. was a great guy and a very encouraging person.

He would come to my office regularly, and every time he talked, he smiled. He would ask how I was and then tell me that he appreciated me. R.C. thanked me for all the work I did and for the opportunity for us to work together. And I would respond that the feeling is mutual. He did it almost every day.

One afternoon when we were talking, I asked R.C. how he could explain his great marriage. I asked him what some of the reasons were for that. (By the way, it is helpful for young couples to have older couples whose marriages are based on Christ to confide in and to learn from.) R.C. said and his wife, Charlotte, practiced the Sweet Sixteen every day when he came home. When I asked him to elaborate, he said they look at each other for 16 minutes and take turns talking and listening.

This is pretty strong advice. But to do this Sweet Sixteen like R.C. and his wife, you have to do what we've already mentioned: get away from technology and prioritize your marital relationship above your relationship with your kids. Taking this kind of time together right after work may not be the best time for you. That's okay. Do it in the morning or before you go to bed or whenever works best for you. It could be any time of the day. Just remember to be time zone sensitive.

Stake out your relational territory in your household as husband and wife and make a daily commitment to take time out to communicate, to share, and to listen.

Most likely, if you are the wife, you are saying, "Oh, I like that." On the other hand, if you are the husband, you may not get this whole Sweet Sixteen concept. Guys, let me put it in our vernacular. Most of us watch sports interviews, right? We see or hear the TV personality thrust a microphone into an athlete's face and ask him a question. Then they ask several follow up questions. In other words, they interview him.

You can do the same thing with your wife. Don't think about the Sweet Sixteen. Instead, interview your spouse. Ask her how her day was. Then ask her several follow up questions. Don't just act like you are listening; dive into her world. Put yourself in her shoes. Women communicate differently than men do; they tend to talk about their feelings first and then the facts. You must ask enough questions to get past the feelings so you can connect.

Identify with what she is saying. Make eye contact. The Bible says, "The eye is the lamp of the body" (Matthew 6:22–24). Pay attention to how you are communicating with your body language, because your body communicates your interest more than your words. Mentally summarize what is being said and then give it back so you can know that you have connected. All these things are huge in communication.

Now wives, you know that guys communicate first with the facts. After you wade through all the facts, you can get to the feelings. That is just the way it is. So, wives, do the Sweet Sixteen, and husbands, do the interview.

James 1:19 says, "Everyone should be quick to listen, slow to speak, and slow to become angry." Studies indicate that seven percent of communication is accomplished with words, thirty-eight percent with tone, and fifty-five percent with facial expressions. Whether these statistics are exactly accurate or not, the overall principle is evident. You can give your spouse spoiled perch by your looks: the eye roll, various facial expressions, and negative body language.

When you are listening, you drive the conversation. Your receptivity allows adequate space for words given, not just the talker. But when you are talking, don't enter what I refer to as "the moan zone." Too many couples just whine to each other. After a steady diet of that, you can smell the spoiled fish. We need to share the tough things, but let's not forget the good stuff too. Let's build and benefit each other.

JUST BECAUSE

Finally, to build and benefit your spouse, give a reason-free gift every once in a while. You could also write a reason-free note. You won't believe what this will do.

During her busy schedule one week, Lisa walked into our church bookstore and purchased a devotional guide just for me. It was a book written by professional fisherman Jimmy Houston, and it was titled *Hooked for Life*. She did it for no reason other than she loved me. The reason I liked it so much was that I could learn about fishing and the Bible all at once. This little gift was perfect for me and meant a lot.

Some good friends of mine told me about one husband who bought a "just because" gift for his wife: a coffee mug with "I Love You" written on it. But the gift goes on. This guy is a neat freak. He gets up at 5:30 am, gets dressed, and before everybody else gets up, he wipes down both cars every morning. He usually makes the coffee, and then he puts this special mug on the table for his wife to have just as soon as she gets up.

For you traditional types out there, how about those good old fashioned, never-fail, reason-free gifts of candy and flowers? Simple thoughtfulness can have a great impact.

Don't forget about notes. With instant access to texting and social media, we often neglect the charm of an old fashioned, handwritten love note. One simple, reason-free note can communicate volumes.

In the past, our pastoral staff would take yearly retreats. We spent a lot of time praying and vision casting. On one of those staff retreats, Pastor Owen Goff, who has been married for many years, opened his suitcase, and out fell eight love notes from his wife, Beverly. We kidded Owen a lot because we were only going to be gone for four days. But we also knew deep down how special those eight love notes were to him.

We have good inspiration for giving reason-free gifts and love notes. If you peruse the pages of Scripture and see how God communicates His love for us, you will see that God has given many gifts to us just because He loves us. The most significant gift is, of course, His Son.

The Bible, without question, is the greatest love note ever written in human history. First John 4:19 says it best: "We love because he first loved us." Let the love example of your Creator motivate you to demonstrate the same kind of love for your spouse.

You may be thinking this advice about creative communication is all good, but what happens when the feelings get frosty? What happens when conversation becomes combustible? What happens when tempers flare? What happens when you have constant arguing going on?

Well, that subject is so important that I have devoted the entire next chapter to how conflict, if handled correctly, can actually help move us closer to our spouses.

The Basics of *Creative* Communication

- Communication is a crucial element that influences every aspect of marriage and requires our best creative energies.

- Take daily technology breaks to improve your time together. Put your phone on silent, turn off the TV and computer, and spend one-on-one time connecting with your spouse.

- Slow down your schedule, saying yes to the best and no to all the rest, so you can enjoy focused time with your partner.

- Practice the "Sweet Sixteen" with your spouse (16 minutes of uninterrupted communication per day).

- Write a "just because" note or give a "just because" gift periodically to demonstrate love for your spouse in a tangible way.

Creative Conflict

DEEPENING YOUR MARRIAGE RELATIONSHIP THROUGH CONFLICT RESOLUTION

3

SEVERAL YEARS AGO, I traveled to Las Vegas, Nevada, to see a world heavyweight championship boxing match. I arrived at the arena about three hours before the big bout began to see some of the preliminary action.

I was mesmerized as I watched all the celebrities pour into the beautiful facility. I happened to notice that right behind me was a man I recognized: the famous boxing referee Mills Lane. He is a fascinating character, with a bald head, crooked nose, and one-of-a-kind voice. He was once an appellate judge, referee, and host of his own television show. Being the shy and introverted guy that I am (I'm being sarcastic), I walked up to him, sat down, and began to talk to him about this brutal sport.

Mills was wearing his boxing referee garb and was preparing to officiate the big fight. I found it extremely interesting to watch him work. He brought the two trained and toned boxers into the center of the ring. Then he went over the rules.

He said, "Okay, I want a clean fight. No low blows, head butting, or excessive clenching." Then he paused, looked at them, and exclaimed, "Let's get it on!" The crowd erupted as the boxers went to their neutral corners, waited for the bell, and then went toe-to-toe as they battled for the prize.

Marital conflict is a lot like boxing. Husbands and wives step into the ring and go toe-to-toe. They throw verbal punches, display fancy footwork to dodge issues, and demonstrate incredible skills of negotiation. The bottom line is that fights, arguments, spats, and brouhahas are inevitable in the realm of marriage.

There will be times when lines are drawn in the sand and sides are taken. With tear-filled eyes of anger and hurt, unresolved conflict leads to separation. You'll find that the two of you will be hugging your respective corners of a king-size mattress that suddenly seems too small.

High emotions may tempt you to put on your gloves and go a few ugly rounds with your spouse in an anything-goes-fight. Head butting, low blows, and excessive clenching will be the norm. During times like these, all you care about is winning, even if it means wounding your spouse.

While driving through a suburban Dallas shopping area filled with stores, coffee bars, and restaurants one day, I couldn't help but notice a myriad of married couples around the complex. I saw some walking arm in arm while window-shopping. I saw others sipping lattés. I saw others sitting on park benches watching a beautiful Texas sunset with beads of perspiration dripping off their noses.

I thought to myself, *What a beautiful sight!* Husbands and wives in different stages of marital development were all enjoying one another. But I wasn't naive either. I knew intuitively that although they looked so kind and sweet on the surface, behind every designer outfit, these couples were sporting some serious boxing gear.

I knew they regularly entered the ring of marital conflict, and I knew they regularly fought over the big four that cause those spectacular fights: sex, finances, children, and work.

Would a professional boxer entertain the thought of stepping into the ring with millions of dollars at stake and a title on the line without being trained and toned? Do you think they'd enter the ring without a general knowledge of the rules that govern boxing? No, they certainly wouldn't.

Yet countless husbands and wives get married and deal with conflict without any training or working knowledge of the general rules that should govern conflict resolution. I want to help change this by sharing with you some ground rules and guidelines about creative conflict resolution. These guidelines hold true in every relationship, but I want to focus specifically on the connection between a husband and a wife.

Now, as I go through these guidelines and ground rules for creative conflict resolution, I do not want you to think for a second that I have a corner on this market. I am a fellow struggler with you. I still have a long way to go in understanding conflict resolution, but Lisa and I have applied these principles over the years, and they work.

Before I dive into these seven guidelines and ground rules, I want you to think about something: your last fight. You may not have had a fight in a long while, or maybe a very recent fight pops into your mind.

What tactics did you use? How loudly did you speak? What nonverbal signals did you give? What issues were batted back and forth? Were any low blows, head butts, or excessive clenching involved? As you think about how you reacted, I want you to consider how you might have behaved in light of the following ground rules.

GROUND RULE #1:
Assess the Damage Prior to Launch

Refrain from launching verbal missiles. Verbal missiles implode on you and your spouse and ultimately hurt the relationship. I realize that it is so tempting to launch verbal missiles. We love those zingers and verbal uppercuts, don't we? Marriage is a process of collecting intimate data. Our spouse shares with us their feelings, thoughts, and struggles, which we download into our spirit. Disarm verbal missiles before they launch.

Here is what happens: in an argument or a conflict, when tempers are flaring and we feel that we are losing, we fire those verbal missiles, manifested often in name-calling. We compare our spouse to the dog, the cat, or some other person. Quite simply, we label our spouse. We compare. Can you believe it? We take this sensitive information that we've downloaded from them during intimate times of sharing, and we use it against them.

A well-aimed verbal missile can halt future growth and destroy a lot of previous gains in a marriage. As satisfying as they might feel at the time, the tough reality is that verbal missiles never serve a good purpose. When verbal attacks are used against your spouse, it will make him or her reluctant to share the kind of intimate thoughts that make a marriage go and grow. You might win the fight, but you'll lose the marriage with this strategy.

I have had the opportunity to talk to thousands of married couples, and I have never had one tell me, "Ed, that verbal missile did it. That one-liner finally changed her. When I called her that name ... And when I told him ..." No, it does not and will not work. Assess the damage before you launch the verbal missile.

A recent study of marital conflict said that one verbal missile can tear apart and take away twenty acts of kindness. It is a 1:20 ratio. That's a sobering thought.

> A well-aimed verbal missile can halt future growth and destroy a lot of previous gains in a marriage.

I try to eat healthy, but my favorite candy bar is a Kit Kat®. During one of my Sunday messages, I ate a Kit Kat and had someone use a stopwatch to see how long it would take me to eat it. I have a huge mouth—my dentist compares it to a town house—so I have plenty of room to work. It took me 23 seconds to eat a Kit Kat, loaded with fat, sugar, and calories. But it took me 20 minutes of intense aerobic activity just to work off that one little candy bar.

> **One verbal missile can tear apart and take away twenty acts of kindness.**

A Kit Kat is like a verbal missile. We can throw a verbal missile out in a matter of seconds, but it may take years to work it off. And even though we can somewhat repair the damage, it sadly leaves permanent scars. So consider your words carefully and recognize the power they wield in your spouse's life.

GROUND RULE #2:
Wave the Banner of Good Manners

Have you ever noticed that verbal missiles are usually loud and intrusive? The gut-level explosive reactions that usually accompany a verbal fight serve not to disarm an argument but aggravate it.

God tells us in Proverbs 15:1, "A gentle answer turns away wrath, but a harsh word stirs up anger." As you are living life together intimately, as you are sharing your hearts (even in conflict), wave the banner of good manners. Why is it that we are often more considerate and kinder to our friends and acquaintances than to our spouse?

Several months ago, Lisa and I were in an argument. I was raising my voice a little bit when the phone rang. Instantly, I transformed from an angry person into a caring, compassionate pastor. "Hello? Oh, everything is great here. How are you doing? Thank you so much for calling. Oh, really? Oh, that is wonderful! Congratulations. When are you due? We will be praying for you. Thank you very much. Goodbye."

After the phone conversation, I went right back into the argument. I had no problem extending courteous and mannered speech to my acquaintance on the phone. I should have made an even greater effort to extend courtesy to my wife, but I didn't. I blew it.

Let's say you had a friend over for some coffee. And let's say you just had brand new carpet laid in your home. Your friend spills the coffee, and the mug shatters. What would you do? Would you say, "Hey, you idiot! You uncoordinated fool! Why did you do that? Do you know how much we paid for this carpet? You are never coming over again."

You wouldn't say that, would you? You would be gracious and say something like, "Oh, it's okay. It's all right. It will come up. Don't worry about that mug. Let's get you some fresh coffee."

Many people think that to change their marriage, they need enormous, miracle-like events to occur. Then, they believe, the ultimate marriage will happen. But that is not the case. I believe that for most marriages to turn into great marriages, it takes small tweaks to move the relationship to higher peaks.

Don't wait for tensions to mount and conflicts to occur before deciding you need to tone down your inflammatory rhetoric. My wife and I have discovered that the key to conflict resolution is what happens *before* the boxing gloves go on, when things are going smoothly.

We need to make a consistent and conscious effort to treat our spouse with respect and courtesy every day. Begin by saying "Thank you" or "I appreciate what you do for me." Be ready to say a simple "I'm sorry" when you know you've blown it. Little acts of service, like opening the door or serving a cup of coffee, can go a long way in building a relational expectation that will ease or even diffuse conflict.

The Bible is clear in Genesis 2:24 that when a husband and wife unite with one another in marriage, they become one flesh. In 1 Peter 3:8, we find these words given to New Testament Christians: "All *of you be* of one mind" (NKJV). As Christ-followers, a husband and wife are not only one flesh through marriage but also one in Christ.

God tells us in no uncertain terms that some serious oneness should be taking place within a Christian marriage. You can't say, "Well, it's his problem" or "It's her problem." No. It's *our* problem.

First Peter 3:8 continues, "Having compassion for one another ... *be* tenderhearted, *be* courteous" (NKJV). The word courteous has the word court in it. When you are courteous and mannerly toward your spouse, you are courting them. What do you do, for example, when your spouse does a chore around the house? Hopefully your first reaction isn't "You missed a spot"? It should be words of appreciation.

Are you waving the banner of good manners? Are you being polite? Your spouse matters to God, and when you treat them with kindness and respect, you are showing that they matter to you too.

GROUND RULE #3:
Stick to the Point and Stay in the Present

It is so easy for conversations, especially heated ones, to drift from subject to subject and completely miss the point. And if we are not careful, they can spiral and tailspin into a crash landing.

The husband walks into the kitchen. The wife spins on her heels and asks for help since the kids are driving her crazy. He replies emotionally, "You are always asking me to help. I am tired and stressed. Do you realize what kind of pressure I am under at work? You are always nagging me—just like your mother does."

The barbs escalate as her emotions heat up. "Don't bring my mother into this! How about you? You are so lazy. You sit there on the couch and skim through Netflix all the time."

The tailspin intensifies. "Channel surf all the time? You just totally ignore me. We haven't made love in six weeks!"

"Made love? Who would want to do that with you? You wear those same stinky college gym shorts every day. You don't comb your hair, and you have coffee breath."

Prepare for a crash landing because we're going down. "Oh yeah? Well, most women would give their right arm to be married to me. I am not going to take this anymore. I'm outta here!" The door slams, and a marriage disintegrates.

How did this happen? It all started with a simple household chore. The wife asked the husband for some help, and from there it, spiraled into a tailspin of communication problems. The in-laws were dragged in, threats were made, and sexual frustration and divorce were mentioned.

This kind of escalation should never occur. We must stick to the issue. If the issue is finances, have solution-driven conversations about finances. If the issue is sex, have solution-driven conversations about sex. Don't mix the issues when you are experiencing marital conflict. Look for solutions, not sucker-punches.

In the heat of the moment, be careful not to bring up every grudge or problem you've ever had with your spouse. Stay with the issue at hand and try to resolve other issues if and when appropriate (preferably at a later time). In this example, secondary issues quickly became accusations and personal attacks rather than an opportunity for resolution, restitution, or reconciliation.

Also, stay in the present tense. Hebrews 8:12 states that God, with respect to His new covenant with Israel, "will remember their sins no more." When we bring up the past, we are doing something God doesn't do. The evil one is the master of bringing up the past, but God's forgiveness frees us up to focus on the future.

Paul, who at one point called himself the chief of sinners (see 1 Timothy 1:15 NKJV), tells us in Philippians 3:13, "But one thing I do: Forgetting what is behind and straining toward what is ahead." God does not want you to focus on your past failures or those of anyone else, especially your spouse. Love and forgiveness provide hope for the future, not fear and condemnation from the past.

Satan may be whispering to you, "Don't let him forget that mistake." "Be sure and bring up the time when she had that problem." But do as Paul asked us to do—forget what lies behind and reach forward to what lies ahead.

One time Lisa and I were in a conflict, and I'm ashamed to say that my selfishness got the better of me. I was so desperate to win the argument that I brought up some issues from our high school dating days. I know, that was a low blow. Don't let that be you. Mature Christian love and forgiveness should compel us to stick to the present and gently deal with the issue at hand.

GROUND RULE #4:
Avoid the Subterranean Level

Too many of us are subterranean fighters. Issues of all sizes and importance arise from time to time, but many of us just bury them. Instead of dealing with them when they first surface, we go subterranean with them. This is another huge problem marriages face in conflict resolution. Learn to face your emotions head-on and share what you're feeling with your spouse. Simply start with "I feel _____ when you _____."

Maybe it is the style of conflict that we saw modeled in our family of origin. "Oh, everything is fine. No problem. Everything is cool. Everything is smooth." Deep inside, though, all these unresolved issues are eating away at us. And as we continue to go subterranean with issues, all that toxic waste begins to leak into every venue and slice of life.

Deal with issues rapidly. Deal with issues when both of you are rested and can talk about them. And deal with them, the Bible says, before the sun goes down. Ephesians 4:26 cautions, "Do not let the sun go down on your anger" (NASB). Forty years ago, Lisa and I said we would commit to that verse. And we have. We settle every fight before we say good night. I know it's hard to believe, but we really do. If we can't settle it, we agree to further discuss it and end the night with "I love you."

That is why I encourage couples to pray together before they go to bed. You'll find it is very difficult to pray together if you are in an argument or in conflict. Many times, Lisa and I have had to stay up almost all night resolving issues, because we don't say good night until we have ended the fight. This is a great tactic, husbands and wives, because it deals with all the toxic waste that is messing up too many of us.

GROUND RULE #5:
Leave the Psychology to the Experts

We have read a few books, taken a few courses, or maybe listened to a few podcasts, so naturally we think we can psychoanalyze our spouse. "Oh, you are being so obsessive-compulsive. You are such an enabler. That is classic textbook stuff." Don't even go there.

Matthew 7:3 is a verse we rarely apply to marriage because it is so convicting: "Why do you look at the speck that is in your brother's eye but do not notice the log that is in your own eye" (NASB)? Jesus was using some hyperbole here, a little Hebrew humor. Just picture it. Here is a husband with a Sequoia tree in his eye saying that his wife has a speck of dust on her contact lens.

When I am critical of Lisa or she is critical of me, we are, in fact, criticizing ourselves, because we are now one. Marriage is not a relationship of dissonance but of harmony. In our egoistical, me-centered world, we have a tough time with the concept of harmony and oneness. The competitive one-upmanship that is so pervasive in our culture cannot and should not find its way into the marital scheme.

Our criticisms and judgments hardly ever serve to build up another person. We use them, instead, as ammunition to make ourselves look better by putting down the other person. Again, remember Ephesians 4:29. Paul says our speech should be "helpful for building others up according to their needs, that it may benefit those who listen."

Are you measuring your words to your spouse according to his or her needs? Or are you spouting off selective psychobabble to meet your own perceived need to feel better and make them feel worse? Skip the psychobabble and concentrate on those crucial words, phrases, and conversations that will build you both up as one flesh.

GROUND RULE #6:
Listen Up Without Winding Up

A lot of us get ready to pounce instead of listening to what our spouse is saying. We do a major league windup and cannot wait to throw the fastball at their head, oftentimes while they are still talking. When we are set to pounce, to interrupt them, it's a sure sign that we are not really listening.

Have you ever been in a conversation where the other person is speaking, perhaps sharing their heart, and you are so busy thinking about what you want to say that you totally miss the message of their words? This tactic isn't good with friends, and it definitely isn't good with your spouse.

When we listen, we should list things mentally to ensure we're tracking with what our spouse is saying. Really listen for the issue at hand. Once we have listed them mentally, we should give them back to the other person for clarification. Now our spouse can indicate thumbs up ("Yes, you got what I said") or thumbs down ("No, you misunderstood").

Proverbs 18:13 cuts to the chase regarding the importance of listening: "To answer before listening—that is [his or her] folly and shame." If you do that, you will never communicate. Conversation—even heated conversation—is a two-way street. You may think you are having a meaningful conversation with your spouse just because you are articulating your concerns to them. But if you are failing to listen to their concerns, then you are not really conversing with them. Listening is showing respect to your spouse and absorbing their feelings about the subject. All you're doing is lecturing them.

GROUND RULE #7:
Make a You-Turn

U-turns are difficult to negotiate, especially if you drive a truck. One Friday night I had the family in my truck, and we were driving around looking at neighborhoods and houses. I got lost, as I typically do, and I had to make two U-turns using people's driveways. It was embarrassing.

In marriage, we need to make another kind of U-turn: a You-Turn. That's because we use the word "you" too much. You. You. You. "You always waste money." "You never talk to me." Instead, we should use "I feel" statements. "I feel that we should save more money." "I feel like we are not really communicating." It changes the whole dynamic, because revealing your feelings is the beginning of real healing in a relationship.

Paul commands us in Galatians 6:2, "Bear one another's burdens, and so fulfill the law of Christ" (NKJV). This is not an optional thing. When you train with weights, you are always encouraged to train with another person so they can spot for you. They make sure that everything is okay and help with the poundage, especially with the last two or three repetitions. A spotter is the best way to go because that person is literally sharing the burden.

Similarly, we are to become relational spotters for our spouses. "Oh, you had a difficult day at work? I want to bear your burden." "Oh, you are feeling down about something your father said to you? I want to bear your burden." It's about sharing and bearing the feelings of another. It removes the "you" factor and reintroduces the "we" factor.

GROUND RULE #8:
Avoid the D-word

The ultimate trump card in conflict is the "D-word"—divorce. Whenever a husband or wife feels really beaten down, this word gets thrown into the mix and usually ends up lighting a powder keg explosion.

Instead of working through the issues or asking for forgiveness, the word divorce is thrown around. "I'm so sick of you. If you talk to me like this one more time, I'm going to divorce you!" That is the fastest way to end an argument but also the fastest way to head for an actual divorce.

Marriage is all about trust. It is impossible to build trust when one or both of you is threatening to dissolve a covenant you made with each other before God. The D-word is often used as a threat to administer pain. We seldom realize the implications of using the word "divorce" and therefore flippantly allude to wanting a "way out." The goal should always be a way *through* rather than a way out.

Let me urge you to never use the D-word. Work on your own junk and seek creative solutions to your conflict. Remember, God is your biggest source of help and your biggest cheerleader when you find yourself in conflict. Ask Him for strength and help to work through your issues in a way that honors Him.

I could go on and on about these conflict resolution principles. You may have even found some others. But the bottom line is that these principles are all found in the Bible, and they revolve around a commitment by both husband and wife to deal seriously, thoughtfully, and rapidly with conflict as it occurs.

THE COSMIC CONFLICT

We have been talking about human conflict so far, but many people are in a seemingly unwinnable and unresolvable conflict that just happens to be the key to all conflict resolution. I'm talking about a conflict with God.

If this is you, you may not want to admit it, but you know deep down what I'm talking about. You have this uneasiness, this sick feeling in the pit of your stomach, knowing that one day you will have to face God and give an account of your behavior.

The Bible says that all of us have made mistakes (see Romans 3:23). All of us have sinned relationally, morally, and spiritually against God and other people. We have violated God's standards. God is holy. He is perfect. Yet we have turned our backs on Him and gone our own way.

While this cosmic conflict appears to be unwinnable and unresolvable, here is what God did to bring reconciliation. Even though He was the violated party, God took the initiative in this conflict. He commissioned His only Son to live a perfect life and then die on the cross for all our mistakes and sins—past, present, and future. And then He rose again.

If we come to a point in our lives when we apply and appropriate what God did for us through Christ, our sins are forgiven, the conflict is over, and we are reconciled to God.

> **When we apply and appropriate what God did for us through Christ ... we are reconciled to God.**

If you have not taken this step, you are in serious trouble. I don't care how good you are, how sweet you are, how kind you are, or how much money you give away to charity or to a church. You are going to fall miserably short of God's standard of goodness. At the end of your life, you are still going to be in conflict with this holy, all-powerful God.

Conflict resolution starts with a step of faith by saying, "Christ, I accept what You did for me and apply it to my life." Your life—including your marriage—will never work if you have not made that decision and taken that step.

I am not talking about religion. I am not talking about a denominational affiliation. Denominations are not mentioned in the Bible. The Catholic Church is not mentioned. The Baptist church is not mentioned. The Lutheran church is not mentioned. Only a decision to accept Christ's gift by grace through faith is mentioned in the Bible (see Ephesians 2:8–9). Have you taken that step? Have you made that choice?

THE MINISTRY OF RECONCILIATION

The moment we receive Christ and what He did for us on the cross, an awesome thing happens. Second Corinthians 5:17–18 tells us, "Therefore, if anyone is in Christ, that person is a new creation. The old has gone, the new is here! All this is from God, who reconciled us to himself through Christ and gave us the ministry of reconciliation." In short, our conflict with God is over because Jesus has taken care of the sin problem on our behalf.

Christ's gift to us is the key to conflict resolution in our relationships with one another. He modeled for us the ministry of reconciliation. If I did not have the ministry of reconciliation and if Lisa did not have the ministry of reconciliation, we would have a rugged marriage. It would not be very pretty. I don't even think we would be married today if it were not for this mutual ministry in our lives.

Lisa and I have a great marriage. I love her more today than I did 40 years ago. And the reason I am able to love her like this is the ministry of reconciliation that God has given to us. Every

> Christ's gift to us is the key to conflict resolution in our relationships with one another. He modeled for us the ministry of reconciliation.

time we have a conflict, we look at what Christ did for us and draw on His presence in our lives to be reconciled to one another.

When Christ comes into our lives, He places the person of the Holy Spirit inside our hearts, and the Holy Spirit gives us the extra power to take action in this ministry. The Holy Spirit will communicate with my spirit. He'll say, "Hey, Ed, quit being so selfish. You have been reconciled to God through Christ, something you don't deserve. Now get on the same page and reconcile with your bride." Lisa has this power operative in her life, too, and that is what makes conflict resolution so awesome for the two of us.

If you don't have the ministry of reconciliation, human nature will dominate with a ministry of retribution. Retribution and retaliation begin to take over, resulting in a barrage of damaging head butts and low blows. These blows serve no positive purpose in bringing restitution or resolution to your relationship. Without Christ, that is what our tendency is as married people. And that is one of the reasons why nearly 50 percent of all marriages are failing right now.

When you have a conflict, take it to God. When you have a relational sticking point in your marriage, talk to God about it. But be prepared for His perspective. Nine times out of ten, when I bring something to God, He says I am the one with the problem. I pray for my spouse every single day. By taking the problems to God and praying for your spouse, you are engaging in the ministry of reconciliation.

If you are ready to get serious with God, you can be a great facilitator in creative conflict resolution. You can do it as you rely on the Spirit of God. But it is a choice that each person has to make. In the next chapter, we will look at intimacy because I am confident that conflict resolution done in a biblical way opens the door to greater levels of intimacy.

The Basics of *Creative* Conflict

- Avoid verbal missiles that harm the deeper, intimate levels of your relationship.

- In conflict, stay on target, stay specific, and stay in the present tense.

- Don't let the sun go down without resolving a conflict. Deal with any issues rapidly. Stay up late and settle the issue or agree to reconcile with a future appointment.

- Settle your cosmic conflict with God and receive the reconciliation He has freely given you through Jesus Christ.

- Offer reconciliation to your spouse in the same way that God offered you the free gift of reconciliation.

CHAPTER 4

Creative Intimacy

REMOVING THE BARRIERS
AND BUILDING BRIDGES
TO A GREAT SEX LIFE
IN YOUR MARRIAGE

4

WHEN YOU HEAR the word sex, what comes to mind? I know the mere mention of that word can bring a flood of thoughts and emotions. But I doubt very seriously that when you hear it, you think about God or any biblical connotations. The fact is, though, you should. God fashioned us uniquely as a male or a female and pre-wired us for sexual desire, and His Word should be our primary guide on thoughts in this area.

One morning, one of my young daughters looked up at me and said, "Dad, when you saw Mommy for the first time, did you whistle?" God has given us this wolf-whistle desire for the opposite sex. He has given us the gift of sex, and He has provided a powerful setting, a valuable venue, to practice and utilize this gift. Contrary to the cues of our culture, sex was created by God to be beautifully enjoyed in the marriage relationship. Throughout this chapter, we will take a look at some "sex busters" in marriage. You may be thinking, *Sex Busters? Isn't that kind of a negative spin on sex, Ed?* And you are right. Normally, I don't like to present the negative side of biblical principles, but in this case I decided to contrast several sex builders with an equal number of positive sex busters.

Sex is a positive, good thing. It is from God, and He wants us to experience great sex. He wants to build a great sex life in every marriage.

However, research shows that one-third to one-half of married couples experience a moderate to major level of sexual frustration in marriage.

What are the hang-ups that serve as sex busters? Sex busters are attitudes or habits that keep us from using this God-given gift in a God-ordained way. On the positive side are sex builders that help you get rid of the things that are keeping you from being the kind of mate, sexually speaking, that God wants you to be. If you want to make love regularly and creatively, you had better deal with this subject matter.

Whenever I speak on the subject of sex, I am amazed at how people pay attention. No one sleeps. No one drifts off into daydreams. No one counts ceiling lights. Some people might think that we should not talk about sex in the church. If that is what you're thinking, you are missing out on what the Bible says about this beautiful gift that God Himself created.

We should not be ashamed to talk about sex. God was not ashamed to create sex and then put it into print. The two most prominent places we should discuss this matter are the home and the church. Historically, the church has done a pathetic job talking about sex. Thankfully, some churches are trying to change that by getting real and talking about what God's Word says on this subject.

The following material is meant for couples who have a relatively healthy relationship. In cases where one party has a problem of abuse or sexual compulsivity or addiction, the personal issue needs to be addressed and treated before focusing on the marriage.

SEX BUSTER #1:
You Don't Know What God Says About Sex

When couples are oblivious to God's take on the subject and unaware of what the Bible says, it becomes a sex buster. The evil one does not want you to have the biblical knowledge, information, and application principles regarding this subject. He doesn't want you to have a great sex life, because if you do, you will bond with your spouse like super glue. In addition, your sexual relationship and connection will provide a foundation for great child rearing principles. The enemy will be defeated.

Most couples are unaware of what Scripture says about frequency, when one person is in the mood and the other is not, romance, and being innovative in the bedroom. "Wait a minute! Are you telling me this stuff is actually in the Bible?" Yes, it is. Read on to find God's answers to these common issues.

SEX BUILDER #1:
Get in Sync with Scripture

When you don't know or understand what God says about something, let me encourage you to search for the answer. This sex builder is that we have to get in sync with scriptural sexuality. There is a huge link between spirituality and sexuality. Couples who make time to express love to God in an authentic way also make time to make love together frequently and creatively.

I have talked to numerous couples who have Christ-centered marriages, and they also have wonderful, mutually satisfying sexual relationships. Study after study shows that the most sexually satisfied people in marriage are those who pray together, read the Bible together, and go to church together. God made sex, and they are doing sex the way He wants them to do it.

> The most sexually satisfied people in marriage are those who pray together, read the Bible together, and go to church together.

First Corinthians 7:3–4 is a foundational passage regarding God's agenda for sexuality in marriage: "Let the husband render to his wife the affection due her, and likewise also the wife to her husband. The wife does not have authority over her own body, but the husband *does*. And likewise the husband does not have authority over his own body, but the wife *does*" (NKJV).

This verse talks about management, doesn't it? Your spouse is the manager over your body. He is. She is. "You are kidding me, Ed!" Look at verse 4 one more time: "The wife does not have authority over her own body, but the husband *does*. And likewise the husband does not have authority over his own body, but the wife *does*." Are you in sync with Scripture? Are you mutually satisfying one another's desires?

SEX BUSTER #2:
You Don't Understand Your Spouse's Sex Drive

I'm going to make a profound statement. Are you ready? *Men and women are different.* I can feel the shockwaves. Thank you, Captain Obvious.

Some couples are clueless about the varying sex drives between men and women. Let's look at the man's sex drive, for instance. A man's sex drive is kind of like a sprint. In an instant, just like that, he is ready to sprint into sex.

A woman's sex drive, on the other hand, is more like a 5K run. She more or less jogs into sex. God has wired us differently with unique sex drives. A husband experiences sex, and from his sexual experiences flow his feelings. The wife is the polar opposite. She experiences feelings before she can experience physical intimacy.

Here is how we mess it up: the husband—the sprinter—approaches his wife the way he wants to be approached. He is aggressive and initiative-taking, and he sprints into sex. The wife, on the other hand, leans on romance that leads to intimacy.

So you've got a problem and some tension going on. You have one party doing his thing his way and the other party doing her thing her way. Get ready because sparks—and not the fun kind—are about to fly as major conflict begins.

SEX BUILDER #2:
Dial into Your Spouse's Sex Drive

Sexual satisfaction is achieved with sensitivity to your spouse's sex drive. Wives and husbands who have it together dial into each other's specific needs.

Let me talk to the men first. For the most part, we desire sex more than our wives desire sex. Now this is not all the time or across the board, but it's true in most situations and circumstances. We know how it is, don't we guys? We make our best move, but she doesn't like it, because she is not in the mood. And we know that sinking feeling we have when that occurs. If you are a man, you know exactly what I'm talking about.

Dr. Willard Harley, a Christian psychologist, has a beautiful illustration that really hammers home an understanding for women of a man's sex drive and what a man goes through when he is rejected. Imagine, a stool with a glass of water sitting on it. The husband is next to the stool, and the wife is next to him. The wife is immobilized. She can't get to the water. The husband is the only one who can get the water.

Here is what happens, Harley says. The wife turns to her husband and asks, "Honey, would you please pour me a glass of water? I am getting thirsty."

The husband turns and responds, "I don't really feel like it. I am not in the mood. Maybe in a couple hours."

Hours roll by. One more time the wife turns to her husband: "Honey, I am getting thirsty. Would you please give me a glass of water?"

The husband responds, "You know, I am kind of tired. I've had a long day, okay?"

Then the wife begins to get angry. She can feel her temperature rising. She desperately wants a glass of water, so she begins to demand it: "I want a glass of water. You are the only one who can give me the glass of water." The husband looks at his wife, spins on his heels, and says, "You are not going to get any water with an attitude like that."

The husband returns to the scene about a day later, and now the wife is livid. Finally, the husband says, "Okay! Here is your water. Just drink it!"

When the wife is gulping down the water, do you think she is satisfied? Do you think her thirst is truly quenched? Not really. She is thinking that she is going to be thirsty again, and if she wants another drink of water, she had better watch what she says to her husband.

So goes a man's sex drive. Like water quenches physical thirst, sex in marriage quenches thirst in a physical, spiritual, emotional, and psychological manner. But sex must be given and received with a right spirit if it is to truly satisfy those longings.

Now let's pick on the men. Men are so compartmentalized and so structured that most of us are clueless concerning the overall context of the marital relationship. We are, for the most part, one-dimensional people.

While boarding an airplane not too long ago, I walked by a group of women. One of the women was reading a book entitled *All About Men.* I looked at her and said, "All about men, huh?"

She said, "Yeah, it's a short book."

I nearly died laughing. As I took my seat about 10 rows back, I said to myself, *I'm going to put that in one of my messages.* The house could be dirty. You could have just been in a major argument five minutes earlier. If you are a man, you are still likely to pat your wife on the rear and say, "Hey, hey, hey. How about you and me head to the bedroom?"

Wives, on the other hand, are multifaceted and multidimensional. The context surrounding the sexual part of the relationship is huge for them. They must know that everything is A-okay outside of the bedroom before everything gets A-okay in the bedroom.

So what do we do about it? Yes, there are those times when the husband and wife are both in the mood, when they both want to make love. But what do you do when one is ready for it and the other is not?

Husbands, here is what you do. You slow down. Quit being a sprinter all the time and jog a little bit with your wife. It's sometimes fun to jog. Wives, don't always run so slowly. Try incorporating some sprints into that 5K. When the husband is thinking about her needs and the wife is thinking about his needs, you'll have two people understanding the pace of passion. If you want to get your partner in the mood, then approach them the way they want to be approached.

> Husbands, slow down. Quit sprinting all the time and jog a little bit with your wife. Wives, try incorporating some sprints into that 5k.

SEX BUSTER #3:
You Have Unrealistic Ideas of Sex

Because of unrealistic portrayals of sex in books, TV, movies, and other media, many couples have unrealistic expectations regarding sex in their real-life relationships.

At Florida State University, a good friend of mine and I would watch movies together every once in a while. Every time he saw something that was lame or a reach, my friend would say, "Ehhhhh, unrealistic." The first few times it was funny, but after the tenth time, it was extremely annoying.

Like my friend—but perhaps in a less annoying way—we need to be identifying unrealistic ideas and images regarding sexuality every time we see and hear them. Virtually everywhere we turn, in every avenue of life, we get hit with this stuff over and over again.

Take our popular, modern day romantic comedies as an example. Sex rarely, if ever, happens in real life like it does on the silver screen. A man and a woman just look at each other, and five seconds later the clothes are ripped off. That is not the way it happens in marriage. So when you see it, just say, "Ehhhhhh, unrealistic."

If the Hollywood crowd had it down cold, then their lives wouldn't be so messed up. If you had to be buff and beautiful to have great sex, then they would have a corner on the market. But you are talking about some seriously messed up people. All you have to do is go through the checkout line at the grocery store and look at the front covers of the magazines to see that these people's lives aren't exactly perfect.

Don't measure your sexuality through the grid of movies, videos, or the secular media. That is not the real story.

Let me also say something about pornography here. It has become somewhat vogue these days to bring adult videos into the bedroom. Husbands and wives rationalize this by saying that watching another couple make love will give them a sexual boost. "What turns them on will turns us on" is the rationalization. I have read the research. Don't buy the lie.

First, when you bring an adult video into the bedroom, you are involved in lusting after and being aroused by another person (or persons). The excuse that you are "just watching" and not actually involved with someone else does not hold biblical water. Christ said that if you lust after someone in your heart, you are committing adultery.

Second, pornography will always get you wanting more and more. You will become addicted to the extra stimulation and will start to need it just to be aroused by your spouse.

Here's some straight-forward advice: if you are involved with pornographic material, trash or delete it and install safeguards on all your electronic devices. And by all means, if you have reached the level of addiction, get help from a good Christian counselor or support group. Pornography has the potential to leave great marriages on the ash heap. If it is not dealt with seriously and swiftly, it will destroy your intimacy with your spouse. Do whatever it takes now to remove this incendiary influence from your life—before it's too late.

SEX BUILDER #3:
See Through the Secular Smoke Screen

See through the secular smoke screen that distorts the realities of a biblical commitment in marriage. Run your love life through the Scripture grid and see what the Bible says about one man and one woman committed to God and to each other in the context of marriage—a man and a woman who are selflessly serving one another with energy and creativity. These couples see sex as an opportunity for greater intimacy and mutual discipleship. In short, it's a win-win for these couples.

After I spoke on this subject at one of our weekend worship services at Fellowship Church, one lady commented enthusiastically to Lisa, "I really enjoyed today's message. My husband and I are going to go home and do some discipleship." Amen!

SEX BUSTER #4:
You Are Trashing the Temple

This sex buster is one of my favorites because it is such an obvious issue and yet something we often overlook. We all need to pay attention to grooming and hygiene issues.

As married men, many of us think, *Hey, I've got my spouse. I can lose the look and gain the weight. I can go on a hygiene hiatus, man. But you should have seen me when I was dating her. Back then, I was looking good!*

Some are so pitiful at this hygiene stuff that they are still walking around with that high school jock look, complete with the same old gym shorts, tattered tank top, and rough, unshaven face. He's thinking, *Hey, baby! I've still got it, you know.* The wife is wondering why she would even want to touch him.

Here is what the wives do. They end up wearing one of those "Not tonight, honey" nightgowns to bed. You know, the kind that screams, "I've got a headache." And they, too, can be guilty of dropping the ball on physical health and fitness. I'm sure you know what I'm talking about.

We can laugh at these humorous scenarios, but they represent a real-life problem in many marriages. After we say, "I do," we often follow it up with "I don't." "I don't need to work hard to look good for my spouse anymore." "I don't need to worry about competing for her or dating her." "I don't have to impress him any longer by taking care of my body."

Being in the ministry is something I absolutely love. There is nothing like it. I see the good. I see the miracles of God as I witness lives being changed regularly. But I also see the other side. I see the results of sin and the devastation of relationships that go astray. And what often amazes me is the physical transformation of someone who is recently separated, divorced, or involved in an extramarital affair. Talk about a transformation!

Sometimes someone who is involved in adultery will come and talk to me about it. I will look at him or her and think, *What happened to you? You have lost 25 pounds. You are dressing cool and have a different hairstyle. I see that you're working for it now with this other person. Why didn't you work for it with your spouse in marriage?*

I will see someone who has just gone through a divorce. She has lost 40 pounds and looks like she just had a total makeover. Why didn't she do it when she was married? While there are some exceptions, and this doesn't necessarily happen across the board, I have to ask myself, *Why did you wait so long to take care of your appearance?* And this isn't just referring to weight gain or weight loss. Physical well-being has to do with energy, mental health, and well-being.

On the way to the airport in another city, I was in a taxi and spotted a sign that read, "It's all about work." This should be your marital bumper sticker. Remember the MWE—the Marital Work Ethic? It takes work to deal with all these sex busters, but it especially takes a commitment of hard work to continue to court your spouse by maintaining your physical appearance. Don't neglect the obvious: you can't keep your sex life in shape if you don't keep your body in shape.

SEX BUILDER #4:
Take Care of the Temple

This sex builder comes from 1 Corinthians 6:19: "Do you not know that your body is the temple of the Holy Spirit *who is* in you, whom you have from God" (NKJV)? Take care of the temple. If you are a Christ-follower, your body is a temple, the dwelling place of the Holy Spirit of God.

We have a saying in Texas: "Don't mess with Texas." Well, God is saying, "Don't mess with the temple." I am not talking about turning into a Ken and Barbie couple or developing a physical obsession that can take over your life. I am saying you should do the best with what you have.

> **When we take care of our body—our temple— we are expressing love to God and love for our spouse.**

Eating properly, working out, and staying as lean as possible are acts of worship to God. Romans 12:1 says to "offer your bodies as a living sacrifice, holy and pleasing to God." When we take care of our body—our temple—we are expressing love to God and love for our spouse.

SEX BUSTER #5:
You Are Making Excuses Instead of Making Love

I have to mention this one because in 1 Corinthians 7:5, the Bible just puts it in our faces. Sex Buster number five is the great refusal. You know what I am talking about. One wants it, but the other says, "No, I'm tired. I'm fatigued. That's all you think about." And most of the time—no offense, wives—it is a situation where the woman is giving those responses.

Let me share with you what happens when you have a negative response to your spouse's advances. First, you can shame your spouse by your response. By constantly turning your spouse down, you are communicating that something must be wrong with his or her desires or that his or her needs are not legitimate. It takes a certain amount of vulnerability to ask for your sexual needs to be met, and it is embarrassing and defeating for that vulnerability to be rejected.

Second, you can mess up your fellowship with God. It is a sin to deprive your spouse of their sexual needs. And any sin puts a strain on your fellowship with the Lord. The marriage relationship is a reflection of the relationship Christ has with the Church. Because of this unique correlation, when your marriage relationship is strained, your relationship with Christ is also negatively impacted.

Third, you are inviting heightened temptations for both you and your spouse. The enemy will use this to draw a partner to look elsewhere for sexual gratification. Nothing justifies a partner sexually acting outside of the marital bed, and the results of doing so can be devastating.

SEX BUILDER #5:
Stop Depriving One Another

In other words, don't make excuses. Make love. "Ed, those are bold words." Those aren't my words. Let's call in the Corinthians. They were having arguments about this back in biblical times, when one was in the mood and the other not.

The apostle Paul, inspired by the Holy Spirit, wrote 1 Corinthians 7:5: "Stop depriving one another, except by agreement for a time so that you may devote yourselves to prayer" (NASB). Aside from certain medical problems or health issues, the only excuse we should give is "I'm in prayer." But you must both be in agreement.

While studying this issue, I spoke with one of our pastors on staff to get his input. This was his take on the subject: "Yeah, if the husband and wife do agree to abstain for a while, I know what the husband will be praying for—sex!" He was kidding ... sort of.

Paul continues, "And come together again so that Satan will not tempt you because of your lack of self-control" (NASB). I don't think the Bible is telling us that we can't ever say no. But no should be the exception. And don't just say no. If you say no, say no with an appointment. "No, in a couple of hours." "No, tomorrow morning." "No, tomorrow night." This appointment gives the two of you something to look forward to.

A big excuse these days is "I'm tired." But for the most part, being fatigued is a mental thing. I love fishing, especially fly fishing in salt water. When I'm on a fishing trip, I can get up at 4 am ready to fly fish. I might be physically tired, but mentally I'm ready to fly fish for tarpon. And that mental attitude helps perk my tired body up.

Too tired for sex? Too fatigued for 20, 30, or 45 minutes with your partner? Mentally tell yourself, *I am having sexual intercourse with my covenant partner. Mentally, I am going to say I am ready.* You'll be amazed how your body will follow this mental commitment.

Here's a hypothetical scenario. The husband and wife are in bed, and she is too tired for sex. Suddenly, the phone rings, and it is her college roommate. The wife is transformed in the blink of an eye from a fatigued female into a fantastic phone conversationalist. "Hi, girlfriend! It is so great to talk to you. What's going on?" Her husband is thinking, *What is up with my wife? How'd that happen so fast?*

It takes two to tango. If you want great conversation, you had better both be involved. If you want great romance, you had better both be taking part. If you want great sex, you had better both be aroused—mentally and physically.

"Well, Ed, are you telling me that I have to say yes a lot?" Yes, I am. That is what the Bible says. And I am not talking about an apathetic "Yes, okay, you can do it." I don't think that's what Paul had in mind. I believe that an apathetic "yes" is as much a sin before God as is refusing your partner's sexual advances.

> It takes two to tango. If you want great sex, you had better both be aroused—mentally and physically.

At this point, if you are a woman, you may be thinking, *I don't like this book at all. This guy is totally out of touch with reality! He is a man, so of course, he is going to say these things.* Well, let me share something with you. Lisa co-wrote this material with me, and she didn't think I was being hard enough on the women. We will come back to this topic in the last chapter, when Lisa and I answer some of the questions we've been asked most frequently about our marriage.

SEX BUSTER #6:
You Are Letting Your Kids Block Marital Intimacy

This sex buster can be summarized in one word: kids. Now, I believe children are gifts from God. But kids can—and will—bust up your sex life. In chapter two, we addressed the need to make your family spouse-centric. This principle is especially important as you consider how to make marital intimacy a priority in your household.

You know what KIDS stands for? **K**eeping **I**ntimacy at a **D**istance **S**uccessfully. If you are not having a regular date night, this sex buster can rear its ugly head. If you don't have regular and enforced bedtimes for the children and certain areas of the house that are restricted during your "romantic hours," your intimate times will be few and far between.

SEX BUILDER #6:
Take a Romantic Getaway

The sex builder is to get on board the 2B-52. B stands for a break, and 52 stands for fifty-two weeks out of the year. Husbands and wives, I challenge you to take two breaks a year just for the two of you. Go away a night or two twice a year, every six months. Go away to fan the flames of your romance. Go away for intimacy. Go away for sex.

"Ed, you just don't know our finances. We can't afford that." Maybe your family can step in to help you with the kids so you can have a little marital retreat at home. Use creativity to make it happen. It is better to pay the price now than to end up relationally bankrupt later on down the road. You don't want to neglect the 2B-52, only to one day find your covenant carpet-bombed and destroyed. Taking these breaks is worth it and will reap huge benefits in your marriage.

SEX BUSTER #7:
You Are Sharing Sacred Stuff with the Wrong People

Do not share those tidbits regarding what goes on in the bedroom with your golfing buddies, your tennis gal pals, or with the person next to you at work. Don't go there.

Pay attention to the words of Hebrews 13:4: "Marriage should be honored by all, and the marriage bed kept pure." Talking with a trusted Christian counselor or pastoral counselor is one thing, but that's where it needs to stop. If you blab this sacred stuff, it will take away trust from your spouse and can fan the flames of adultery.

SEX BUILDER #7:
Discuss Sex Openly with Your Spouse

The person you should be having a sex talk with is your spouse. Sit down and share your likes and dislikes, wants and desires, problems and needs. Put everything on the table and deal with it.

Maybe you need to go through a book on sex like "Restoring the Pleasure" by Drs. Cliff and Joyce Penner. You could read aloud one chapter a night together or read it separately and each of you highlight your favorite passages to discuss later. You won't believe what can happen.

If you're uncomfortable talking about sexual matters, then start slowly until you can develop a mutual comfort level for heart-to-heart sharing. The greatest part of sex is communication, so you need to find a way to bring communication into the marriage bed.

SEX BUSTER #8 (FOR SINGLES):
You Are Dabbling in Premarital Sex

I've studied many of the major world religions over the years. One thing I've found in each of them, without exception, is a clear teaching against premarital sex. The downside to casual sex is so obvious and damaging that the collective wisdom of all faiths agrees on this point.

Regardless of what other belief systems say, though, there is no room for premarital sex as a single Christian person. You are committing treason before God. It does not matter if it is with your fiancée or someone you have known for a long time. If you are living together and sexually involved, you are sinning before God. I understand the temptation and allurement that must be fought daily to continue to live a sexually pure life, but when you live in sin, God cannot and will not bless your present life or your future sexual life in marriage like He desires.

You may try to convince yourself that it's no big deal, that it's only a physical thing, and that it won't impact your future relationship. But premarital sex is not just a casual or physical thing. It is a multi-faceted, multi-dimensional part of the total relationship. There are spiritual, psychological, and emotional aspects to sexual intimacy.

When you involve yourself in premarital sex, you have a great chance of marrying the wrong person. Why? Sex is so powerful that it can blind your reasoning abilities. Sex bonds you together unlike anything else. You will hook up with him or her and later think, *Why in the world did I do that?* It was probably because you had intercourse with him or her.

If you are having sex now outside of marriage, stop. Stop! Say that you are going to unwrap the greatest gift possible for your spouse on your wedding

If you are having sex now outside of marriage, stop. Stop! Say that you are going to unwrap the greatest gift possible for your spouse on your wedding night: your sexuality.

night: your sexuality. Don't lie to yourself, and don't fool yourself. God ordained sex for the marriage bed for a reason, and we need to respect the fact that despite what we might feel, God has our best interest at heart. You need to go to Him for strength in this area. Trust Him to meet your needs while you wait for your future spouse.

I have a close friend who lives on the West Coast. He was a college athlete, and during those college years, he was very promiscuous. He later became a Christian and got married.

After several years, his marriage was going through horrible problems and hanging by a thread. He was getting ready to do something that was so stupid I just could not believe it. By the grace of God and through some confrontations from his Christian friends, he and his wife sought Christian counseling.

Thankfully, they got back on track and are now doing great. But he would be the first to tell you that the reason he had those issues in marriage was because he was so promiscuous before marriage. It was like he brought all those other girls into the bedroom with his wife.

Don't do it. It is not worth it. I know sex is fun, and that's true of all sin—at least at first. But sin not only has kicks; it also has kickbacks. And the kickbacks are brutal.

SEX BUILDER #8:
Keep Yourself for the Covenant

This point is pretty self-explanatory. If you've messed up in the past or are in the process of messing up and messing around, stop now and save yourself for your spouse. If you've been disciplined enough to keep yourself from premarital sex, don't give up. I know it's hard.

The temptation can seem unbearable at times, but God will reward you for your faithfulness. Do whatever it takes to preserve this sacred act and reserve it for marriage.

Avoid tempting places and situations, like being alone together in your apartment or car. Date publicly, with preset boundaries that will work for you in keeping God's covenant purpose. Consider some group activities where you have accountability in numbers. And follow Paul's advice to the Corinthians: "Flee from sexual immorality" (1 Corinthians 6:18). It's that simple.

When you're tempted to give in to sexual sin, run. Get out of there. Don't deceive yourself by saying, "Oh, I can handle it. I'm not going to give in to these urges." God knows how hard this area is for us, so He warns us to get out when the fire starts to get too hot.

SEX BUSTER #9:
You Are Stuck in Monotony

You've heard about a monogamous relationship, right? That's a good thing. Well, there's something out there called a *monotonous* marriage that is not such a good thing. In fact, it's a big-time sex buster. This marriage consists of the same old, rut-like relationship. You've got the same old look, wearing the same old wardrobe, talking the same old talk, stuck in the same old place, and engaged in the same old love making.

Instead of monotony, we need to model our lives and relationships after the essence of God. God is not monotonous; He is highly creative and innovative. If we know Him, live for Him, and worship Him corporately and individually, we are going to have creativity in every area of our lives.

You can't do the same things the same way and expect unique results. We have to change. We have to work. We have to kick monotony out and do sex like God wants us to.

SEX BUILDER #9:
Bring Back the Romance

If you look up the word impractical in the dictionary, one of the synonyms is romantic. Don't you like that? We have to become impractical people of romance.

Guys, we need help in this area, so here is a challenge. Take a modern translation of the Bible and read Song of Solomon in the Old Testament. Talk about some hot stuff! It is written to husbands and wives concerning lovemaking and how to keep romance in a relationship.

Solomon was creative. He couldn't even spell monotony. Solomon made his wife earrings. He wrote her poetry. He paneled the master bedroom by himself with fine wood cut from the cedars of Lebanon. He took her on long walks through the forest.

What did his wife do? Did she respond to his creativity with monotony? No, she didn't. She approached him the way he wanted to be approached. And he approached her the way she wanted to be approached.

The text says she danced before him in a sheer negligee. It says Solomon took her to a biblical bed and breakfast. Solomon's wife took the initiative and said, "Solomon, let's make love outdoors. I want to show you something old and something new." I'll stop there. You can read the rest for yourself. The B-I-B-L-E, that's the book for me!

When I opened this chapter, I asked what you think about when you hear the word sex. It is my prayer that from now on you will think about God and the biblical connotations Lisa and I have outlined in this chapter. We want you to do sex His way, within His parameters, and use this amazing gift the way He desires. Thank God for that audacious, incredible desire for the opposite sex. Let's build great sex into our marriages by following these sex builders and eliminating those sex busters. Have fun!

The Basics of *Creative* Intimacy

- Look at sex the way God intended, taking cues from Scripture rather than our culture.

- Get in sync with your spouse's sex drive and talk openly about your sex life.

- Take care of your body as an act of worship to God and out of honor and respect for your partner.

- Implement creative date nights and take your 2B-52 getaways to fan the romantic flames of your relationship.

- If you are single, make a commitment to save sex for the marriage bed. Unwrap the greatest gift you can give your spouse on your wedding night.

CHAPTER 5

Creative Finances

DEFENDING YOUR MARRIAGE AGAINST THE MONEY MONSTER

5

LIKE MOST YOUNG married couples, Lisa and I spent our first years together in an apartment. Three years after we added a couple dogs to our family (one a 140-pound Rottweiler, and the other a 70-pound mutt), we decided it was time to look for a house.

We searched throughout the Houston city limits and found a 35-year-old home. We bought the house because it had a big back yard and because we could fix it up over time. And sure enough, we lived there for several years.

I'll never forget the first time we ever decided to do yard work. I don't really like yard work that much, so Lisa had to coax me to get out of the house and into the backyard.

There was an old tree house in the left portion of our backyard that was in pretty bad condition. Not paying much attention to this eyesore, I started the mower and began to mow the lawn.

In the midst of mowing some pretty nice lines through our lawn, it happened. I found myself surrounded by dozens of bees and was stung three times. I am talking about major league stings. To make matters worse, I am allergic to bees. Needless to say, I began to dance and jump around like I was auditioning for a dance contest. I ran inside and said, "Lisa, bees ... everywhere ... stung ... ouch ... allergic ... ouch!"

With all the compassion in the world, she said, "Honey, you probably just got stung a couple of times. Maybe it was just a random thing. Go back and keep mowing the lawn."

Like a good husband, I went back and cranked the mower again. This time the dogs started yelping and rolling around on the lawn. The bees had found a new target: my two poor dogs. There were bees all over them. I ran inside again. "Lisa, more bees. Dogs got stung. This is a major ordeal! I have an idea. Why don't you go back outside, Lisa, and you start the mower up, and maybe we'll find the source of these bees."

I dressed up my lovely wife in a sweatshirt, pants, and hat. She looked pretty good. The only things you could see were her eyes. She walked out, and when she cranked the mower, a swarm of angry bumblebees leapt out of the old, dilapidated tree house and began to attack Lisa. Big surprise, right? Although she was impervious to the stings because of all the protective clothing she had on, she was running around, and the dogs were yelping again.

Lisa finally charged into the house. I opened the door from the safety of our home, and she ran inside. I closed the door, but it was too late. About 10 bees were now inside the house and were hitting the windows. We had a serious problem on our hands. After a tense battle, we finally managed to kill the bees that made their way into our house, but there was still the matter of the angry bees in our beautiful backyard.

Lisa got on the phone and called a man who specializes in outdoor pest control. This man was a great guy named Mr. Smith. Mr. Smith walked with a limp since he had injured it during the Vietnam War. We explained that we had an angry hive of bees in the tree house, and he advised us to just calm down and let him handle the situation. He said, "I have dealt with bees for the last 15 years. Bees won't sting me, because I know their habits. And I have this special formula."

Mr. Smith came over and climbed a ladder so he could peer into this tree house. The bees attacked. He fell off the ladder and started rolling around. The bees were so aggressive that he sent them off to a lab at Texas A&M to see if the bees were killer bees. He told us that these bees were the nastiest ones he had seen in his 15-year career.

It is definitely scary when you are attacked by bees. I've been there, and maybe you have, too. I want to address something in this chapter, that is even scarier, though. Have you ever been stung by killer *fees?* That's right, killer fees. It doesn't matter if you make billions, millions, thousands, or hundreds of dollars; if you are married—or single—you are going to be attacked in one form or another by these killer fees.

Just like hunting down the source of a beehive, the first thing we need to do to protect our finances is to discover the source of these killer fees. Much research has uncovered that many divorces or issues in marriage are over finances. It is a major problem and a major source of conflict in marriage.

Gallop once estimated that 56 percent of divorces in our country are due to conflicts and arguments over finances.

When you think about killer fees, you have to think about their three-fold strategy of attack. What do killer fees do?

- They sting us.
- They immobilize us.
- They wreak havoc on us.

To combat this attack strategy, we need to understand the following three major sources of killer fees.

ATTACK OF THE PLASTIC PIRANHAS

The first source of attack is in the form of plastic. Do I need to explain what I am talking about? Credit cards. You get married and begin to use credit cards to buy certain "necessary" items. You know, like the new smart phone or one of the millions of subscription services available now. When this type of spending becomes a regular habit, just watch and see what happens.

Credit cards are interesting little things. They come in pretty, shiny colors of red, white, and blue, gold, and platinum. You can buy beautiful nature pictures or have your favorite sports team plastered all over the card. They have our names engraved on the bottom of the card and even how long we have been card members. And they have the most prominent display case in our wallets.

They seem painless to use at first. In fact, when you use some cards, you get frequent flier miles and discounts on automobiles. The banking world loves for us to use credit cards. You buy something, hand the credit card to the store clerk, the clerk runs it through a computer, gives you back the card and says, "Sir, will you please sign your name right there?" You sign your name, and no problem, you have the item. Quick and painless.

As you go on your merry way, you thinking to yourself, *Man, a credit card is the way to go. I love this little card. It's my friend.* However, 30 days later, you bring the mail in, and you hear a muffled gnawing sound. And you think, *Could there be mice or termites in our house?* Then you open the envelope and look at the bill in your hand. Yes, that persistent sound of gnawing and gnashing is the precursor of an imminent attack of the killer fees. You are being stalked by the dreaded plastic piranhas. They smell blood.

A recent television commercial advertising a particular credit card actually warns us of this imminent attack. Have you seen this one? A man comes home to his wife after having bought a particular item with a credit card. She asks him, "You bought this stuff with the credit card? Do you know what those interest charges are going to do to us?"

As she's saying this, a deadly mob of barbarian warriors is descending the hill toward them, ready to ravage, loot, and plunder their home. The genius of the commercial is that the couple avoids the pillage because the husband used one of those cards with a zero percent introductory rate. The barbarians are disappointed to have to skip their home, but they are seen going after the neighbors, who recently bought something without this "special" credit card.

Don't be deceived; don't get mocked. The couple in this commercial is only delaying the inevitable. Introductory rate or not, credit cards will get you in the end, because most of us use credit cards to buy things with money we do not have.

Studies show that Americans who have credit cards spend 26 percent more than those who do not have credit cards. The Bible warns in Proverbs 22:7, "The borrower *is* servant to the lender" (NKJV). Money becomes a slave trader, selling us up the river to a lender who gains mastery over us.

We have two options with credit cards, and I want to challenge you to apply these options. The first option is to pay them off every month. Credit cards should be a tool of convenience, not a financial mechanism for getting now what we can't afford.

The second option is more drastic but necessary to many of us. Take a giant pair of scissors and cut your credit cards up. Some of you need to get serious about this because your finances are out of control. Instead of having your money work for you, you are working for your money. It is literally running away from you. You have no clue where your money is, and you are overextended. You are in major league debt because of these shiny credit cards and their ability to purchase things so easily and painlessly with money you don't have.

It is just too easy to hand that shiny card to a cashier. This kind of transaction makes you feel like you aren't really spending. That is the reason why those of us with credit cards spend that extra 26 percent. It's time to wake up and face the reality of what these cards are doing to you and your family.

Several years ago, a financial consultant reminded me about the warning that appears on a pack of cigarettes. He said, "Ed, you know on those cigarettes there is a little Surgeon General's warning that smoking is hazardous to your health?" He continued, "I think that we should put little stickers on every credit card that would read, 'Warning: Overuse can be hazardous to your wealth.'" I agree with him. If you have or need credit cards for some reason, fine. Just make sure you pay them off every month. And if your finances are out of control, cut the credit cards up.

The Bible doesn't tell us never to borrow money. I have heard people say, "Well, the Bible says time and time again never to borrow money." What the Bible does speak against is borrowing money and not being able to pay it back. In Psalm 37:21, God has harsh words for the person who does not pay his debts: "The wicked borrow and do not repay." We should be cautious borrowers by borrowing as little as possible, only when absolutely necessary and only when we can pay it back.

Never let debt spin out-of-control, because it will begin to rule and run your life. And there is no kind of pressure that compares to being under the gun financially. You'll literally cringe every time you head for your mailbox. I promise you.

> There is no kind of pressure that compares to being under the gun financially.

The world talks about financial security and for good reason. Christians need to talk about and live out the principle of stewardship. Everything belongs to God. God owns the sun, the stars, our cars, and our homes. We need to get it in our heads that we are managers of all the stuff God owns. If those plastic piranhas in your wallet are attacking you, then it's time to fight back.

THE MEDIA BLITZ

Another source of killer fees is the media. The American Association of Advertising estimates that the average person in our society sees or hears over 10,000 commercials or advertisements a day—on the radio, television, billboards, and a myriad of other places.

Advertisers hire the best producers, the best writers, and the best actors to participate in these commercials with one goal in mind: to create discontent. They want the viewer to say, "I have to have that." "I need to buy that." "I can't live without that."

Advertising is a trillion-dollar industry. That's right, *trillion*. Why? Because it works. They are succeeding in creating discontent in our society, even among Christians who should know that contentment can't be purchased at department stores or online.

Jesus said in Matthew 10:16, "Be as wise as serpents and harmless as doves" (NKJV). We need to take our cue from the cunning nature of the snake. When you see a commercial, let me challenge you to look at the un-pictured, hidden side of the advertisement.

For example, let's consider beer commercials, which must be the most creative commercials on TV. One of the classics features a cool guy with about three percent body fat. He drives his $125,000 shiny sports car up to a bar and steps out. He walks into the bar, and people greet him like he's the life of the party. Beautiful women come up to him and kiss him on the cheek, and he says, "Yes, I'll have a such- and-such beer." The bartender sets him up with this special beverage, and the voice-over announcer says, "It doesn't get any better than this."

What is that commercial saying? It is saying that if we drink this beverage, we can drive a $125,000 sports car, have three percent body fat, and have all these beautiful women kissing us. We will have a lot of friends and be the life of the party. Sounds easy enough, right? Maybe we should all be buying this product. But what this creative commercial is not showing you is the hidden reality that their product will never be a key to helping you achieve the physique, status, and wealth you desire. The dark side of these products is that they often actually prevent you from achieving your desired goals. Whenever you watch a pleasing commercial like this, train yourself to look past fantasy to the reality of what they're selling. Don't be deceived.

How about car commercials? You will see these cars zigzagging through the Swiss Alps and you think, *Man, I've got to have that new car because it has this new sound system, it has the latest technology, and it even has massagers in the seats! If I could only have that car.* It is fine to drive the car, but once again, look at the un-pictured reality. I'll bet the payment book will be as thick as the Bible—and I'm not talking about a pocket-size Bible either. I'm talking about the Bibles with four translations, commentary notes, and 30 pages of maps! Listen again to Jesus' warning: "Be wise as serpents and harmless as doves."

THE PEER PRESSURE PRESS

A third source of the killer fees is peer pressure. I like the word peer because it communicates a word picture of peering at each other to see what the other person has. And scrolling mindlessly through social media gives us instant access to see how others live. "They have that home. They drive that car. They are members of that club. I am just as educated, I'm just as smart, and I'm the same age. I deserve it just as much as they do!"

We have this never-ending cycle of the "gimmies." We compare and classify ourselves, and we think, *I must have that.* Numbing out on the tenth commandment (thou shall not covet), we rationalize our desires by telling ourselves that we deserve this or that just as much as our neighbor does. Have you ever used these excuses before?

How did this materialistic mentality take hold in our world today? America is definitely the most materialistic, money-hungry nation on the planet. But why?

Let me give you a typical example of Alex, the average American child. As Alex grows up during his impressionable years, most of the conversation he hears around the breakfast table centers on money—where it can get you and what it can buy for you. He concludes that money really does talk.

Then he sees his father climb up the corporate ladder, and because his father is climbing the ladder, he gets raises. Alex's family moves across the country to a bigger house. And then they get an even bigger house; always up scaling and living to the max of their financial means. Alex thinks, *Well, I guess money is more important than spiritual roots, family roots, or relational roots. Sounds good to me. Where do I sign up?*

And then Alex, the average American child, finally grows up. He talks to his parents about college, and his parents say, "You need to go to that university and major in that subject because it will yield the highest income. Even though you might not like the field that much, you'll forget about that when you're swimming in your sparkling swimming pool."

Alex graduates, gets involved in a high-power career, makes a lot of money, gets married, and begins to pass on, unknowingly and unwittingly, this same value system he learned from his parents to his own children.

As an elderly man, Alex looks back and discovers that his whole life has been focused on the pursuit of the money monster. He has been led around through life on a short leash, oblivious to this struggle. It can happen. It is real. And I see too many of Christ's followers being led around by this materialistic, money-driven mentality.

THE BUDGET BLOCKADE

How do we take care of these methods of attack? How do we fend off the plastic piranhas? How do we dodge the media blitz? How do we hold up under the peer pressure press? Let me give you four strategies to fight off these three common temptations.

One repellent has been shown to be effective time and again against the killer fees. It is not that Raid bug spray. It is spelled B-U-D-G-E-T. I want to address the importance of a budget, because the Bible says we should live on and follow a budget.

First, when you set a budget, pray about it with your spouse. "What, you mean I should actually pray about my money? I have never prayed about my budget." We need to do this because everything we have comes from God, so God needs to be involved in all decisions regarding our resources.

You might say, "Well, I am a self-made man" or "I am a self-made woman." Ok, let me ask you a question: who gave you the drive to succeed? Who gave you the initiative and talent? All of it came from God. He is the One who blessed you with these incredible gifts. It is because of His sovereignty and grace that you are where you are. Never forget that.

Pray about your finances as a couple. "God, where do You want us to spend our money? What do You want us to do? Where do You want us to put limits and where do You want us to be really generous?"

> Agree together about some goals for saving, some goals for spending, and some goals for giving.

Set some mutual goals. I think there are at least three areas for goal setting. Agree together about some goals for saving, some goals for spending, and some goals for giving. Have you ever done that? A couple times a year Lisa and I sit down together and hammer out a budget. We then live by that budget and have a good time abiding by it, because it's something we have agreed on together. When our daughter and her husband were first married, they established a once-a-month budget date night. This discipline helped them plan and execute a successful financial future. This process can be laborious and tedious, but the payoff (pun intended) is worth it!

FIRST THINGS FIRST

What kind of budget should we have? We should live by the give-give-live budget. This is a biblical budget. The give budget is setting aside at least 10 percent of what you get paid for God's work. The Bible says you should give it to your local house of worship. The Bible is plain about this concept. It is called tithing.

Every time I deliver a message about giving, I see those who are generous, and they are kind of smiling and thinking, *Yeah, that's great, Ed. I agree with you. Preach on.*

And those who don't give are thinking, *Whoa, you're talking about money again? I'm going to find a church that never talks about money!*

The first thing I'd say to that person is beware, because any church that doesn't address money issues is not teaching the Bible. Jesus talked as much about money as He talked about heaven or hell. How does that strike you? The second thing I'd say is just relax. God doesn't want you to give grudgingly or out of obligation. The truth is, He doesn't need our money. He is all-powerful and totally sufficient without our help.

The Bible says we should be cheerful givers (see 2 Corinthians 9:7). If you are a cheerful giver, then God is going to take care of you and bless your life. He may bless your financial situation. He may bless you with strong and vibrant relationships. He may choose to bless you with great health. God promises to bless generous and cheerful givers throughout Scripture. In Proverbs 3:9–10 we are told, "Honor the Lord by giving him the first part of all your income" (TLB).

You see, the amount is insignificant. If you make a million dollars a month or if you make ten dollars a month, the Bible says that the first part—the best part—should go to God. Why? Does God need our money? No, God doesn't need it, but He uses money to test us and see if He really is Lord of our life. When we hoard our money, we are showing God and others that we think we are the master of our own domain.

Giving also allows you the incredible opportunity to be involved in God's eternal work in the lives of people. Jesus said, "For where your treasure is, there your heart will be also" (Matthew 6:21). If your money is going to God's work, your heart belongs to God. If your money is going to purchase more and more stuff, your heart belongs to the ad agencies.

We can look at our financial portfolios and tell what or who is number one in our lives. It doesn't take long at all. Is it travel? Is it clothing? Is it a home? Is it a car? Or is it the Lord Jesus Christ?

A lot of people wonder why God doesn't bless their finances. Why doesn't God give them opportunities? Why doesn't God do this or that? Oftentimes, it can be traced back to the lack of generosity and the lack of giving to the local church.

God promises to bless those who give to His work. Look at the entire passage in Proverbs 3:9–10. "Honor the Lord by giving Him the first part of all your income, and he will fill your barns [or your condos] with wheat and barley [money, new job] and overflow your wine vats [health, great relationships] with the finest wines" (TLB).

God talks more about giving than any other subject in the Bible, because when we give, we become more like Him. The first part of John 3:16 says, "For God so loved the world that he *gave*" (emphasis added). As we give, we are being conformed to the character of the greatest Giver of all.

Do you have the crippling disease called cirrhosis of the *giver?* When you get paid, give the first 10 percent to God. It will bless your life, your marriage, and your family in ways (financially and otherwise) that you can't even imagine.

THE PERSONAL PAYBACK

After giving the first 10 percent to God, we give the second 10 percent to ourselves. Of course, I'm talking about the biblical concept of saving money.

Have you ever seen fire ants? We have some major fire ants in Texas. They're big here, and they're everywhere. Fire ants are interesting creatures, and you would do well to just take a step back (a big step back if you know what I mean) and watch them. Consider Proverbs 6:6: "Take a lesson from the ants, you lazybones. Learn from their ways and become wise!" (NLT).

The wise fire ant gathers and saves stuff, but it does not have a leader, a CEO, or a coach. The proverb continues, "Though they have no prince or governor or ruler to make them work, they labor hard all summer, gathering food for the winter" (vv. 7–8 NLT). In other words, the ant lives on less than it gathers and puts the rest away for a later time when the gathering will not be as easy.

I recently read that the average European saves 16 percent of his annual income. The average Japanese man or woman saves 25 percent of their annual income. The average American saves 4 percent of their annual income. Only 4 percent. As Americans in a materialistic society, we need to tone down the consumerism and tune into a saving and investment mentality.

As you begin to save and invest, you will learn the principle of contentment. The Bible says repeatedly that when we live God's way, we will experience contentment. We should be content with the contents of our life. We need to say, "God, I want to live on a margin, so here is my budget. I'm giving my first 10 percent to You and the second 10 percent to myself." And the remaining 80 percent is what you get to enjoy. So live it up!

> **As Americans in a materialistic society, we need to tone down the consumerism and tune into a saving and investment mentality.**

THE ENJOYMENT FACTOR

God loves to give you gifts, and He loves to give me gifts. Money is not the root of all kinds of evil. The Bible says, "The *love* of money is a root of all kinds of evil" (1 Timothy 6:10, emphasis added). Money itself is neutral. The question is, do you own your money or does your money own you?

If your money owns you, then you are not really enjoying it. God's plan is for us live on and enjoy the remaining 80 percent. Are you enjoying it? Proverbs 21:5 warns, "The plans of the diligent lead to profit as surely as haste [credit cards, impulse buying, spending because of peer pressure] leads to poverty." Enjoying your money requires diligence and the ability to master it, rather than it mastering you.

Have you ever been to Target before? The answer is most likely yes. And if you ask a lady in your life how she feels about Target, she will most likely say she loves it and she may be "obsessed." Maybe it's the big, bright red circle or the cute little dog they use as their mascot or, most likely, that there is a Starbucks in almost every store. But for whatever reason, ladies love Target.

And when there is a sale at Target, get ready to clean out some closet space, because your whole home is about to be redecorated. "With what, exactly?" you may be asking. And the honest answer from ladies is "We don't know. Target tells you what you need." Suddenly, they are back at home with bathrobes and Christmas lights in the middle of August, just because they got caught up in impulse spending. If you spend with haste, it leads to poverty, even if it is "just a quick trip to Target."

And don't think I'm picking on women. Guys also get caught up in impulse spending, and when they do, it's often on a larger scale. Rather than bathrobes, they are more likely to come home with a big-ticket item like a riding lawnmower or the newest technology. There's nothing wrong with buying these things if you can afford them and if they are within your give-give-live budget. Live on 80 percent and enjoy it but live wisely and diligently with your discretionary income.

Almost everyone in the United States has an automobile, and each of those sedans, sports cars, SUVs, and trucks has a gas gauge (unless you're driving an electric car). What if I told you to go home this afternoon, take a hammer, smash the gas gauge, and drive with a smashed gas gauge for a year?

Would that be fun? "Whoa, I'm not sure how much I have in here. I don't know if I should floor it, ease off the pedal, or fill up the tank." You would run out of gas before you know it, because you wouldn't have any idea how much gas was left in your tank.

This would cause you to get pretty frustrated and upset, saying words you don't really mean, getting angry, kicking the dog, and yelling at the kids. A lot of us spend our entire lives without a spending gauge—no perimeters, no boundaries, and just 129 easy payments away from bankruptcy and a total loss of control. It is my prayer that you will let God's principles of budgeting—giving 10 percent, saving 10 percent, and then living on and enjoying the rest—be the gas gauge in your financial life. If you will take these biblical finance principles that Christ talked about more than He talked about heaven or hell and apply them, God can and will do great things in all areas of your marriage and personal life.

The Basics of *Creative* Finances

- Don't let credit cards enslave you and your spouse. Either pay them off every month or destroy them.

- Pray and plan for a budget that will help you meet your giving, saving, and spending goals.

- Bring back to God His 10 percent.

- Pay yourself the next 10 percent in savings.

- Enjoy the remaining 80 percent!

CHAPTER 6

Creative Priorities

KEEPING YOUR FAMILY
SPOUSE-CENTRIC INSTEAD
OF KID-CENTRIC

6

THE STATEMENT WAS made early one morning in a local coffee shop. A toddler-toting mom was sitting in a comfortable chair and talking to another woman. I was sitting just a few feet away, minding my own business as I studied and did some research on marriage and family issues. While sipping their morning brew, these two women engaged in deep dialogue.

It always amazes me how women are able to share their emotions and lock in on a conversation no matter who's around. I was sitting right next to these women, but I could tell they were oblivious to me. When the conversation turned to parenting, I naturally could not help but listen in. The toddler-toting mom was talking about the challenges of childrearing and how to maintain a good marriage with her husband's busy travel schedule. The other woman, between sips of her coffee, was discussing whether she and her husband were even mature enough to have kids.

After a while, I just couldn't take it anymore. I said, "Excuse me, ladies." They turned and looked at me like, *Oh! Someone is sitting there? Someone else is here besides us?* I said, "Do you mind if I ask you a couple of questions? I'm doing some research on marriage and parenting." They said, "Sure." As I began to probe a little into their particular situations, they opened up and shared some of their concerns about marriage and family. After a while, it was time for me to head to the office, so I packed up my things and headed toward the door.

As I was leaving, the toddler-toting mom turned, looked at me, and made a statement that I will not soon forget. She said, "You know, I think I'm a great mom but not a great wife."

As I thought about that statement, it occurred to me that many parents today would echo the same frustration. I think many would say, "You know, I'm getting the parental job done pretty well. But the spouse thing still needs a lot of work." In this chapter, I want to focus on that statement made by the toddler-toting woman in the local coffee shop. I believe it is critical to understand the tension expressed in this statement if we are going to have the kind of marriages God wants us to have.

There is an important underlying question found within this woman's statement. By expressing the frustration that she is a better parent than spouse, she is asking, "Should my home be a kid-centric home? Should all the activities and all the stuff and all the scheduling revolve around my children? Or should my family be a spouse-centric unit where the marriage takes precedence as the ultimate priority? Which one do I put first?"

The kid-centric family is popular in modern American society. This funnel cloud began to take shape during the sixties and seventies. After World War II and the baby boom, well-meaning modern parents turned their backs on the Bible and rejected advice from their parents. Instead, they put their stock in people like Dr. Spock. (I'm not talking about the man of Star Trek fame. I'm talking about the man of permissive parenting fame.)

Dr. Spock and other permissive parenting persuaders said, "The home should be a democratic institution. Everybody is equal. There's no real leader." They said, "Parents, crawl into the playpens of your rebellious toddlers, sit Indian-style, and try to reason with them." It sounded so vogue, so hip, so cool, so modern. And liberated parents everywhere bought into this philosophy, hook, line, and sinker.

There is just one problem with that kind of philosophy: it doesn't work. All you have to do is take a quick panoramic view of the homes, schools, and playgrounds of your community to discover that this permissive parenting style has some major flaws. Go to a restaurant with a kid-centric family to see these flaws up close. This kid-centric pattern is tempting, and I've been down that road a few times myself. But here's what happens when you put your child at the center of your solar system and revolve everything around him or her.

Let's say a young man and woman who are deeply in love get married and have a few kids. The wife steps down from her career, and her number one priority—being a wife—changes to being a mom. In essence, she marries her children. Conversely, the husband steps down from his number one priority—being a husband—and marries his career. Now he chases promotions and money. For the wife to get to her husband, she must negotiate through a maze of work responsibilities and meetings. For the husband to get to his wife, he must negotiate around all the needs and demands of his children and possibly her career.

The ramifications of this shift in priorities are numerous and costly. You have a marital drift taking place as you begin to lose touch—emotionally, spiritually, and physically—with the person you married. It can seem like you are merely sharing a house as roommates, rather than sharing lives in a one-flesh relationship. You have resentment because the children are demanding all your time and energy, and at the same time, your basic marital needs are not being met. All of this gives way to anger, and you begin to say explosive and hurtful things to each other out of frustration. Throw an attractive neighbor or co-worker into the mix, and you have the potential for some major marital trouble.

This funnel cloud of the kid-centric home has been picking up speed over the past several decades and is spinning out of control. Families today are cranking out rebellious, selfish, sassy, and irresponsible children. Sadly, the same funnel cloud has been leaving wrecked marriage after wrecked marriage in its wake.

This was not God's design for the family. We are to love our kids. We want the best for them. But we must understand that making our children the center of the family universe is not in their best interest, and it is certainly not in the best interest of the marriage relationship. From the very beginning in Genesis, the obvious biblical priority in the family unit is marriage. Marriage must take priority over every relationship in the home.

Parenting is the process of teaching and training your children to leave.

I know this book is about marriage, but to help you understand why a spouse-centric home is best for everyone (including the children), I want to share with you my working definition of parenting. Parenting is the process of teaching and training your children to leave.

I didn't pull this definition out of thin air. It comes straight from the principles found in God's Word regarding parenting. Let's pull apart this definition and look at each facet of our God-given responsibility as parents.

The teaching element comes from Deuteronomy 6:7: "You shall teach them diligently [them being the commandments of the Lord] to your children, and shall talk of them when you sit in your house, when you walk by the way, when you lie down, and when you rise up" (NKJV).

The training piece is found in Proverbs 22:6: "Train up a child in the way he should go, And when he is old he will not depart from it" (NKJV).

And we discover the leaving part all the way back at the very beginning in Genesis 2:24: "A man shall leave his father and mother and be joined to his wife, and they shall become one flesh" (NKJV).

Children are supposed to leave, and parents are supposed to stay. Thus, the marriage should be at the top of the family food chain. Have you ever wondered why there are so many twenty-somethings and even thirty-somethings still living at home? It's because their families have been kid-centric for so long. They've felt the warm spotlight and have been in the starring role for so long that they don't want to leave.

> **If you want to build a mutually satisfying marriage and be a great parent at the same time, your relationship with your spouse must come first.**

The parental co-stars are doing all the work, and the stars are getting all the perks. At eighteen, they say to themselves, *Hey, this is a sweet deal! I get a free room, free laundry service, and incredible meals. Plus, I can work, make a salary, and have a lot of money to spend.* The kid-centric family funnel cloud keeps rolling along.

In chapter two we talked about the fact that you will have approximately 18 years with your children, and then you will have the rest of your life with your spouse. You are not benefiting anyone by focusing on the kids to the detriment of your marriage relationship. If you are not parenting your children to leave and cleave, you are missing the boat with them. And if you are not nurturing your marital relationship, you are drifting away from the one person with whom you will be spending the rest of your life. You are facing the very real prospect of living out your post-parenting years in a home with a person you don't know anymore.

I'll put it as plainly as I know how: if you want to build a mutually satisfying marriage and be a great parent at the same time, your relationship with your spouse must come first. After all, the Bible compares Christ's love for the Church to a husband's love for his wife. Children aren't mentioned there. Friends are not used in comparison. Now, I love children, and I know you do, too. But it's all about the husband and wife, because everything else in the home flows from that biblical priority.

Let's look at some of the things we need to do to have a spouse-centric household, because that's what God wants. In order to attain this ultimate destination for our marriages and families, there are several destinations we need to travel through. If we are going to really understand how to change our family, our community, and our culture, we must follow the right road map toward a biblical household that places the marriage relationship above our relationships with our children. As you trust God and His way for the family, He will reveal a successful rhythm for your marriage and your kids that will help you thrive over the long journey ahead.

ATTENTIONVILLE

The first destination is a place called "Attentionville." Let me ask you a question: do children need oxygen? Sure they do. But if you give them too much oxygen, it will smother them. How about attention? Do children need attention? Sure they do. But if you give too much attention to them, it will smother them. Kid-centric families are in the danger zone of smothering the children. Parents like these will say, "Oh, what do you want? What do you need? Don't cry; here's some candy. Here's some money. Where are we going to eat? You tell me."

Twenty-four hours a day, seven days a week, these parents are giving maximum attention to their kids. You may be thinking, *Oh, that's what I'm going to do for my children. That sounds good.* The problem is, the marital math doesn't work when the kids are getting all your time, attention, and emotional resources. We must intentionally schedule the attention we give our children in certain time increments, with the established priority of the marriage relationship.

When we first had children, Lisa and I made the choice to make our family spouse-centric, and I'll tell you how it played out in our home. I usually arrived home by 5:30 or 6:00 pm. I walked in the door and greeted the kids by giving them kisses and hugs. Then I usually proceeded directly into the kitchen. Most of the time, Lisa and I would spend some time talking in the kitchen, so I'd turn and say something like this to the children: "For the next 20 or 30 minutes, don't come into the kitchen. Your mom and I are going to talk. Now, if there's bloodshed, come in. Other than that, you just go and play."

Sometimes they would try to cry and moan because they wanted my attention. But I believe this kind of routine teaches them that Mommy comes first to Daddy, and spending time with her is Daddy's priority. It also teaches them autonomy and responsibility. It teaches them how to separate and individuate. It communicates in a real-life way, "Hey, I'm a part of a spouse-centric home."

I talked to a close friend of mine a while back about this whole spouse-centric idea. He said, "Ed, you know what we do? After the evening meal, my wife and I have our children clean up the mess. While they're doing that, my wife and I walk around the neighborhood and talk. Invariably, my children will say, 'Can we hang with you, Mom and Dad? Can we walk with you? Let us go, please!' We turn and say, 'No. This is our time. We love you, but Mom and Dad need some time alone together.'"

Don't miss the importance of this first destination. Attention-ville is a place you need to travel through, not a place you set up camp. Our kids need us to spend a certain amount of time there every day, in rhythm with the time you spend with your spouse. I'm all for spending quality time with my children. I loved my kids when they were young, and I love them now that they are adults. I love the time we now have with our grandkids, but we still have to do it in a scheduled manner. You never outgrow the fundamental truth that our focus starts with setting aside consistent and intentional time with our spouse first. You do not have to create some militaristic, ultra-strict schedule, but certain time increments must be maintained if you are going to achieve the rhythm of a spouse-centric household.

NIGHT-NIGHT-VILLE

There's another destination we need to travel through to create a spouse-centric household, and I have written a song to illustrate this special place. I'm a frustrated songwriter and singer, and I made this song up when the children were little to help them get ready for bedtime.

Let's all go to Night-night-ville.
There we will get very still.
It's time to go to Night-night-ville.
So everyone can chill.

Now, this song was not that popular around our household, but Night-night-ville is the next destination we must travel through on a daily basis. "Ed, I get it. You're telling me bedtime is important. Of course, our kids go to bed every night. That's not that big of a deal." This doesn't just mean getting your kids to bed whenever they get tired or feel like going to bed. I'm referring to a structured and patterned bedtime.

Look at Deuteronomy 6:7 again: "You shall teach them diligently to your children, and shall talk of them when you sit in your house, when you walk by the way, when you lie down, and when you rise up." A structured bedtime is one of the important ways you can teach your kids about God and His Word.

Set up a routine for putting your children to bed every night. You can spend time reading Bible stories and praying. Make sure it is understood that after the routine, it's lights out. And here's the kicker: this established time is not for their benefit—it's for yours. Don't put them down when they are ready. Put them down when *you* are ready. Take a step back with your spouse and ask, "Okay, how much time do we need to connect at night? How much time will that take?" Then do the math.

When our twins were five and our son was eight, Lisa and I put them to bed between 7:45 and 8:00 pm. That may sound pretty early to you—they could have stayed up later than that—but we established this time for our benefit, not theirs. As they got older, we reevaluated their bedtime and let them stay up a little later. Even though they were getting older, they still needed that structured time of rest, and we still needed that time together in the evening as husband and wife.

"Well, Ed, you don't understand. I've got a teenager." So did we. To our teenagers we would say, "You can stay up until 10:00 or 10:15, but around 9:00 we want you to cruise to your room and hang out there until bedtime." It showed them, once again, the priority of the spouse-centric family. It said that Mom and Dad have something special going on. It's very tempting to let your teenager set his or her own schedule, but you need to maintain control while giving them some freedom and flexibility.

Now, let's assume you've done that. You've had a few navigational errors but have finally arrived in Night-night-ville. I know this is not an easy thing, so you should be congratulated for arriving at this important family milestone. Let's say your children are in bed, your teenager is invisible in his or her room, and you and your spouse are alone together. Even with the kids in bed and no distractions, something may be keeping you from maximizing this exclusive time together. A virus has been contracted in many marriages that keeps a lot of homes from being spouse-centric.

In the early 2000s, an infamous "Love Bug" virus attacked computers all over the globe. The virus was so devastating that Wired Magazine wrote a story decades later describing what happened: "Once infected, the victim's computer would send an email to everyone in their contacts with a copy of the virus, disguised as a file titled 'love-letter-for-you.' Faced with such a tempting message, many people took the bait, opened the attachment, and got infected." Millions were impacted globally, British Parliament was shut down, and financial institutions came to a screeching halt. All because someone created a virus that exploited people's desperate desire to be loved. Well, there's another virus that's worse than the Love-Bug. It's the Marital Love Bug, and it's trying to infiltrate homes like yours and mine.

Here's how it plays out. It happens when you're alone, as a husband and wife, after the kids have gone to Night-night-ville. You finally have a little free time, a little quiet time, so you decide to start texting, catching up on emails, or perusing social media. This is one of the major ways the Marital Love Bug can attack your home. Keep your social media, texts, and calls to a minimum during this time so you can concentrate on connecting with your spouse. Lisa and I take a phone break several nights a week just like we did when we were parents of toddlers or teenagers. Just place your phones on "do not disturb" or put them in another room and walk away. It's a great thing. Now, I'm not saying you should never use your phone at night, but you need to intentionally minimize distractions that keep you from focusing on your spouse.

Something else that causes this virus and messes your connection up is housework and office work done in the home. "Finally, the kids are in bed. I have some quiet time to go to my study and finish up this project or to prepare for next weekend's message." Or "I can finally finish dusting or cleaning the kitchen or mopping the floor." Now and then, there are some exceptions, but for the most part you should not use up this quality time to finish up chores or do work stuff. If you must, then set a time limit. Make an agreement with your spouse that you will each spend an hour doing some work and then devote the rest of the evening to being together.

The next way the Marital Love Bug gets into your home is the biggest problem. This virus can contaminate your marriage through a little device called a remote control. Many, many couples spend their evenings with the remote, all the while thinking they are spending time with each other. "We just binge watch shows together, Ed. That's what we do. Watching TV together is our favorite pastime." Let's be honest: when we consume content on TV, we don't care what our spouse is doing. We are not really doing anything to connect with him or her. We're just into the sitcom, movie, YouTube video, or news program that has our attention.

Watching some TV or videos on your computer or phone is fine, but for the most part, it's a vast wasteland of garbage. Something powerful happens when you give your spouse priority over a screen. Once you begin to get serious about warding off the Marital Love Bug virus by limiting your screen time, you will begin to make some serious eye contact with your spouse. Suddenly, especially if you are a man, you will find yourself talking to your mate in complete sentences. Imagine the possibilities, guys. There's no telling where these complete sentences might lead! I can hear the excuses already: "Oh, man, I just can't go a night without watching Netflix and ESPN." Yes, you can. Trust me—you'll thank me later.

As you contemplate the importance of Attentionville and Night-night-ville, consider the words of 1 Corinthians 14:40: "But be sure that everything is done properly and in order" (NLT). You must be committed to regular, scheduled time with your spouse, or else it won't happen. If you are not proactive about this, the kids will vie for all your attention, the Marital Love Bug will bite, and you will discover one day that you have drifted apart.

DATEVILLE

Let's travel to another location: Dateville. I've been talking about this particular destination for years now, and you will find me hammering this concept repeatedly throughout this book. I encourage couples to date at least twice a month. I'm referring to a date where you and your spouse go out alone.

When I have the opportunity to speak around the country to leaders or pastors, usually during a Q-and-A they'll ask me a question like this: "Ed, tell me about your personal life. What's the most important thing you do to have a healthy family?" I always say, "No question, the most important thing in my family is my date night with Lisa." In the early days of our marriage, we installed a date night into our schedule, and it revolutionized our connection. It's like an oasis, oftentimes in the middle of the week. It's the greatest thing we have ever done for our marriage!

During one particularly busy time in our lives, Lisa and I went about four weeks without a date night. I was doing some speaking, and we were both doing some traveling. We could sense that marital drift was beginning to take place. If you aren't having a regular, strategic date night, please begin this routine now, this very week.

> It's like an oasis, oftentimes in the middle of the week. It's the greatest thing we've ever done for our marriage!

I know you may be thinking, *Yeah, that sounds good, Ed. Sounds great in theory, but what about the real world?* I can attest to the fact that it's not just a good theory, but it can also be done. Don't put it off. Hire a babysitter. Just have a standing sitter for a certain night or a certain day. If you don't want to do that, then trade off with your friends. The date does not have to be at night. A good friend of mine has "day-dates" with his wife. He has a day off in the middle of the week, so they have breakfast and lunch together and just spend time together during the day. Look at what works best for your schedule, and then be creative about making it fit.

I really have to laugh when parents give excuses like, "You know, we would love to have a date night; we really would. But you see, our children just will not stomach a babysitter. They throw fits and tantrums, and they cry. And you know, Ed, for that matter, we would love to go to Fellowship Church every weekend, but they just don't like it when we leave them in the nursery or preschool or in FC Kids area at church."

These parents may not realize it, but what they're really saying is, "Hey, we don't run the show. Our kids do! We're kid-centric. They rule. They reign. They're the stars, and we're the co-stars. Oh, whatever you want, baby. Oh, don't cry!" Please, it's good to let your kids cry sometimes. It's good to leave them from time to time. It teaches them separation. It teaches them the priority of marriage. It teaches them that Mom and Dad always come back. This is a healthy thing.

Let me throw in something else for extra credit. Parents, I challenge you not to allow your children to sleep with you. Now, if there's an infant in the bassinet in the same room, that's fine. If the child has gone through some traumatic situation, has a nightmare, or is sick, then every so often it's okay if they sleep with you. But if this becomes an "every night" occurrence, the lesson being taught is this: our bedroom is just another family space rather than a sanctuary for Mom and Dad.

When you have a family, the first step to a great sex life is establishing boundaries with your kids. "This is a special place that Mom and Dad have. This is our bed. Your bedroom is right down the hall, so you sleep there." As you begin to teach the importance of separation within the home, it helps your children when you leave them in the nursery, the kids' area at church, camp, or with the grandparents. Now and again, you're going to have to fight some battles, but it is well worth it. That is just extra credit, kind of a side trip off Dateville.

ACTIVITYVILLE

If you are beginning to feel a little convicted at this point, this next one is going to take it up a notch. You may even feel a little defensive, like I am stepping on your toes and meddling with your life. "No one's going to tell me how to raise my children! I can't believe some of the things he wrote about Attentionville, Night-night-ville, and Dateville."

I learned something a long time ago about myself. Every time a man or a woman teaches the Bible and the Holy Spirit convicts me of something, I usually have that same reaction. I say, "No one's going to talk to me that way. This person doesn't have the right to tell me what to do." And usually, when I have that kind of knee-jerk reaction, it means "Ed, you need to make some changes." So here we go to the one of the most difficult destinations.

The next destination we need to travel through is Activityville. We're burning our children out in many ways, with soccer, baseball, basketball, cheerleading, voice lessons, dance lessons, art classes … the list goes on. I am all for extracurricular activities. I am into athletics. I value art and dance and all that good stuff. There is nothing wrong with kids being involved in competitive activities. I am all for these things, but the keyword is *rhythm*. You must regularly and objectively evaluate whether these extracurricular activities are throwing off the rhythm of your family. Are they drowning out your ability to make your spouse your first priority ?Are all these activities truly benefiting your kids? These are tough questions you must ask.

A while back, my wife and I had dinner with a world-class, multi-sport professional athlete. Over the appetizer portion of this meal together, this man looked at Lisa and me and said, "You know, I will never let my children play children's athletics or get too involved in extracurricular activities. I want them to enjoy being kids." Now, I do not know if I would go that far. Such a restriction is a bit extreme and may be driven by some negative experiences from his own childhood. But I certainly understood where he was coming from. We need to allow children to be children, and over-scheduling them can take away from that carefree, childhood experience.

I think it is good for children to play in leagues to a certain extent. Between the ages of six and eleven, however, we must be careful about pushing them too far too fast. Ask yourself this question: *Why do I want my child to play in or be involved in this activity?* Is it because you are an F.A.A. (Frustrated All American)? There's a little F.A.A. in each of us. "You know, if I hadn't blown my knee out, I would probably be in the NFL right now." No, you would not. Let us just face the facts, okay? You are not in the NFL because you were not good enough! "Well, if my voice teacher hadn't been such a snob, and if she hadn't liked Heather instead of me, I would be a star." I am sorry to rain on your vocal parade, but no, you are not on tour right now, because you are not that talented of a singer.

The problem with children's athletics is that adults set the leagues up, adults schedule the games, and children play for the approval of their parents. Take soccer, for instance. Have you ever gone to a little league soccer game? During one soccer game, my son was playing goalie. E.J. was having hard time focusing at various times during the game, as little kids often do, particularly when the action was down on the other end of the field.

E.J. was down there by himself, skipping rope, looking at flowers, and pulling up blades of grass. Meanwhile, I was on the sideline yelling, "E.J., get in the game, man! Pay attention!" And then I thought, *What am I doing? He's just a little boy doing what little boys do.* We must keep things in perspective and take the pressure off these kids to constantly perform and compete.

Do not misunderstand me by thinking, *Well, Ed said our children can never play athletics or get involved in activities.* I'm not saying that. It's got to be your decision before God. In Matthew 6:33, Jesus said, "But seek first his kingdom and his righteousness, and all these things will be given to you as well."

Are you a Matthew 6:33 family? Can you keep the pace you are at with your current lineup of activities and sports and still be a Matthew 6:33 family? That's the rhythm you need to achieve as you make your way through Activityville. I can't make the call for you. You've got to make it yourself.

I hear this from parents all the time: "Oh, yeah, we love the church. We want to develop our marriage. We want to develop our relationship with Christ and be a Matthew 6:33 family. But our kids cannot go to the student program at the church because they have a select soccer practice every Wednesday. They can't get involved in the children's camp or the student camp, because they already have a tournament scheduled. Sundays at church are too hard to make because of the late game on Saturday or the early game on Sunday."

You have to make the choice to establish and maintain the rhythm God has for your family. The moment activities begin to encroach upon your development as a husband and wife, and especially upon your relationship with the local church, you know it's time to take the next train out of Activityville.

> **The moment activities begin to encroach upon your development as a husband and wife, and especially upon your relationship with the local church, you know it's time to take the next train out of Activityville.**

Remember the statement made by the toddler-toting mom? "I'm a good mother but not that great of a wife." If that statement is true for you—if it resonates with you— then you need to navigate successfully through each of these destinations: Attentionville, Night-night-ville, Dateville, and Activityville. On the other hand, you may be able to say, "Ed, I really think I have a spouse-centric home." If so, I hope you will use this chapter as a reminder to keep that rhythm in your home. I know it has been a good refresher course for me. The pressures on the family are constant. We need to fight for our family by continuously evaluating our commitments against our priority of being a Matthew 6:33 family. When we make the decision to follow the right map toward the right destinations, we can look forward to reaching the ultimate destination of a loving and spouse-centric household.

CREATIVE PRIORITIES FAMILY TEST

The following quiz is designed to help you evaluate, in a practical way, how you are balancing the priorities of marriage and family. Answer each question as honestly and accurately as you can by circling the appropriate number (1 = Never, 2 = Sometimes, and 3 = Always). Then add up all the numbers you circled to get your total score. A scoring explanation is included at the end of the quiz.

1. Do you go on a date with your spouse at least twice a month?

Never	Sometimes	Always
1	2	3

2. Do you eat dinner as a family around the dinner table at least three times per week?

Never	Sometimes	Always
1	2	3

3. Do your children sleep in their own beds (not your bed)?

Never	Sometimes	Always
1	2	3

4. Do you and your spouse have TLC (Touch, Look, Conversation) on a daily basis?

Never	Sometimes	Always
1	2	3

5. Do you get away for a weekend alone as a couple (without your kids) at least twice a year?

	Never	Sometimes	Always
	1	2	3

6. Do you have sexual intimacy with your spouse at least two times a week?

	Never	Sometimes	Always
	1	2	3

7. Do you and your spouse present a unified front when your children question your authority?

	Never	Sometimes	Always
	1	2	3

8. Do you have a set bedtime for your kids/teens that is consistently enforced?

	Never	Sometimes	Always
	1	2	3

9. Do you regularly evaluate your calendar to prevent ECA-itis (over-scheduling Extra-Curricular Activities)?

	Never	Sometimes	Always
	1	2	3

10. Is weekly church attendance (age-appropriate worship/teaching) a priority for you and your children?

	Never	Sometimes	Always
	1	2	3

Total Score: _____

– If you scored 10–17, your marriage and family are way out of rhythm. Although you have good intentions, your priorities need a major tune up.

– If you scored 18–24, you are somewhat out of rhythm. As a married couple and as parents, you need to fine tune your priorities based on the principles from this chapter and throughout this book.

– If you scored 25–30, you should have written this chapter instead of me. You have a family that has a healthy rhythm. Continue to challenge yourself to follow God's design for your marriage and family.

The Basics of *Creative* Priorities

- Marriage is God's top priority for the family. A great marriage is the best gift you can give your children.

- Parenting is the process of teaching and training children to leave your home, cleave to a spouse, and weave a family of their own.

- It is possible to smother our children with too much attention. The attention we give them must be in proper rhythm with the priority of marriage in the home.

- A weekly or semi-monthly "date night" will revolutionize your marriage and family.

- Schedule at least one entire night free for family time and at least three meals around the dinner table each week.

- Each season, evaluate the extra-curricular activities (ECAs) of your family and make sure they are not encroaching upon the top priority of your marriage or your family's connection to the local church. Try to limit each child to one ECA per season.

CHAPTER 7

Creative Harmony

RECREATING MARRIAGE
AND FAMILY AFTER
DIVORCE

7

IT'S AMAZING TO realize that only about one-third of the households in the United States reflect the traditional nuclear family unit. Whatever generation you grew up you can likely see evidence of how the family has changed dramatically in pop culture, your neighbors, and most likely even in your own family. Most of America's families are now predominantly single-parent or blended families. Because of this overwhelming majority, I felt compelled to include a chapter in this book on the delicate but very real issues of divorce, remarriage, and the blended family.

Before I get into the challenges of recreating marital and family harmony after divorce, I want to go all the way back to the beginning and look at God's model for marriage. Whether you are marrying for the first time or are in the process of remarrying, you must understand that God's original intent was for one man and one woman to come together in a marriage covenant.

After we look at God's model for marriage, we will address God's concessions for divorce. People ask me all the time, "Ed, what does the Bible say about divorce? When is it biblically okay to divorce?" I am also going to answer those questions in this chapter. I want to assure you up front that if you are divorced, there is hope for you. God is a God of second chances, and that includes remarriage.

Finally, after considering the biblical grounds for divorce, we will hit the home stretch by taking a look at the unique struggles of trying to start over again. How do you know when it's time to remarry? What do you need to be aware of as you consider another potential mate? How can you make a harmonious new family out of so many dissonant parts? The term "blended family" is something of a misnomer, because the blended family is anything but blended in the beginning. It is my intention to show you that there is hope for you to experience harmony and unity in your new relationship as you ground your new marriage and family in the ways of the Lord.

GOD'S MODEL FOR MARRIAGE

As we consider God's design for marriage, what better place to start than in Genesis 2:24? This whole concept is summed up in a neat little package: "A man leaves his father and mother and is united to his wife, and they become one flesh." You would think, at first glance, that the closest relationship on the planet would be a blood, parent-child relationship. But that is not the case, because God says in His Word that something powerful and magnetic transpires when a man loves a woman.

A man and a woman—don't miss this—are going to leave the close blood relationships of their father and mother, and they are going to get together in something God calls "marriage." And then, God tells us, a one-flesh

> The Hebrew term for "one flesh" means to be melted together, to be inseparably linked.

relationship will occur. The Hebrew term for "one flesh" means to be melted together, to be inseparably linked. What once were two separate parts have become one unified component. You can't get the pieces apart.

Think about what happens when you mix green and yellow Play Dough. No matter how you try to pull the two colors apart, the green Play Dough will always be part of the yellow and vice versa. That is what happens when two people come together in marriage. God says there will be so much trust, love, vulnerability, and commitment in this one-flesh relationship that it will be the greatest human relationship in the world.

Now let's allow our minds to wander back a little bit farther to the garden. Adam and Eve had a great marriage. Like everything else in God's creation, it was created perfectly. That is, before sin entered the world. Adam and Eve were sensitive to one another and to God. They had tender hearts. When God would say, "Adam, take care of the animals," he would respond, "Yes, Lord. I love You, Lord." Adam was obedient, and he enjoyed a special, intimate relationship with his Creator. When God said, "Adam, take care of Eve" and "Eve, meet Adam's needs," they would do it. Everything was flowing perfectly in this God-designed relationship.

Something happened that destroyed this pristine environment. Adam was made as a creature in the image of God with the freedom of choice, and he chose to rebel against God. He said, "God, I'm going to pave my own path. I am going to forge my own future. I'm going to eat this fruit off this forbidden tree. I'm not that concerned about this silly rule." The moment he did that, he exchanged his tender heart for a concrete heart. And because of Adam's sin, we have all inherited that same concrete heart and rebellious spirit. In short, we are for us and against God.

Do you remember when you dated your spouse? Think back to that time for a moment. When you dated your spouse, I'll bet you were pretty sensitive to him or her. I know that Lisa and I were very sensitive. We had these special nicknames. Lisa used to call me "Pumpkin," and I called her "Princess." Our favorite song was "Get Closer" by Seals and Croft. Wow, that's a blast from the past, isn't it? When something would happen to damage the relationship, even if it was just a slight misunderstanding, we would come together very quickly. "Oh baby, I'm sorry. Did I hurt you?" You were tender-hearted, weren't you? The last thing you wanted to do was to hurt the other in any way. Everything was flowing, growing, and going.

Then you got married, and things began to change.

Let's just consider an average American couple. For the purposes of this illustration, we will name the husband "Cal Concrete," and the wife "Kim Concrete." This average American couple decides to get married. They have a lovely ceremony and go on an incredible and romantic honeymoon. After the honeymoon is over, the months and years roll by, and they begin to get into a pattern. An insignificant thing happens one day, and they get into a little argument, a fight, but they don't really reconcile. Over time, little arguments like these build up, and the tension slowly but surely builds. One day, it all blows up in their faces. Cal and Kim have a major argument with years of unresolved baggage spilling out. Ugly and regretful things are said.

Cal and Kim Concrete have drifted apart because of the sin of unresolved conflict in their relationship. Once this crack starts to appear, the Evil One begins to widen it until it becomes a giant chasm. The Evil One jumps into the cab of a giant cement truck, backs it up to Cal Concrete, and deposits a load of cement into his spirit, causing him to develop a concrete heart. Cal has turned from being tender-hearted and sensitive to one hard-hearted dude. He crosses his arms defiantly and says, "If she thinks I am going to come back to her, that woman has another thing coming. I'm waiting for her to apologize for all the things she has done to mess up our marriage. I don't care what the Bible says about taking the initiative. It's her fault, so she's the one who needs to make it right!"

At the precise moment this exchange is taking place, the Evil One pulls up to that cement truck and deposits a load of cement into Kim's spirit. Now she, too, is burdened with a concrete heart and says something very similar to what her husband said.

However, the Evil One is not the only one working. While this chasm is forming between Cal and Kim Concrete, the Holy Spirit is waging His own battle. He is whispering, "Hey guys, you forgot Ephesians 4:32: 'Be kind and compassionate to one another, forgiving each other, just as in Christ God forgave you.' Let Me soften your hearts toward one another by giving you the power of forgiveness and reconciliation."

Cal chooses to ignore the soft voice of the Holy Spirit, and one day, he notices an attractive girl at work. He says to himself, *You know, I bet she's sensitive. She looks better than my wife, and I can tell she's sweet.* An emotional attachment begins to form, and then a physical relationship develops—adultery. He is entangled in an extramarital affair. Because of a weak attempt or no attempt at all at reconciliation, this husband becomes another statistic. And the same thing is likely to occur with Kim. She sees a man, gets emotionally attached to him, and steps down the path of adultery and divorce.

The Evil One feeds Cal and Kim many lies. "Hey, go for that relationship. You will really be satisfied over there with him! You want to be happy, don't you? Let him meet your emotional needs. He is the one you were meant to be with in the first place." The Holy Spirit, though, is still there whispering, "Remember, the relationship between the husband and wife is a picture of Christ's relationship with the Church. It is about the covenant and commitment, and it is there for life." And on and on it goes, back and forth.

The story of this average American couple sounds familiar, doesn't it? It sounds so biting and so real because it happens every day. You see, God knows we don't live in a spiritual utopia. He knows we don't live in a perfect world. God is well aware of our predisposition to develop concrete-like hearts, and He knows we are going to mess up and make marital mistakes. But even in the middle of those mistakes and hard-hearted episodes, God's model is one man and one woman together forever in marriage. He has provided the spiritual tools through the Holy Spirit for us to work through those marital foul-ups and experience reconciliation. We have been discussing those various tools throughout the pages of this book. Sometimes, though, the mistakes are so egregious that reconciliation seems impossible, and we feel that we are left with only one option—divorce.

GOD'S CONCESSIONS FOR DIVORCE

God boldly proclaims in Malachi 2:16, "I hate divorce." However, Scripture has allowed some concessions for divorce. The model is one man and one woman, but I am going to share with you three biblical grounds for divorce. I give you these three grounds with caution and only after spending countless hours in research, in discussion with theologians, pastors, leaders, and scholars over decades of ministry. I must caution you not to look at these three grounds as a way out or an escape clause of the marital covenant. "Oh boy, I finally have a reason to ditch this person." There is no fine print in this marital covenant.

> **God says, first and foremost, that you need to look for a way through instead of a way out.**

God says, first and foremost, that you need to look for a way through instead of a way out. So many people today are ready to throw commitment out like a sack of trash. They throw away trust, and they throw away love, asking themselves, *What's in it for me?* as they jump from one relationship to the next.

However, when Christian counseling has been used and prayer and hard work have been exhausted, God has granted three grounds for biblical divorce and remarriage. The first concession is found in 2 Corinthians 5:17. This passage, I believe, indicates that we are free to remarry when a divorce has occurred prior to establishing a personal relationship with Jesus Christ. The apostle Paul writes, "Therefore, if anyone is in Christ, that person is a new creation (with the exception of divorce)." Is that what it says? No. It says, "Therefore, if anyone is in Christ, that person is a new creation. The old has gone [that means divorce, peddling drugs, illicit behavior, or any other sin we could possibly think of], the new is here!"

The word "new" in the original language means new in form and quality. If I divorced prior to my salvation, prior to my personal relationship with Jesus Christ, the Bible says I am free to marry again. I am free to make a fresh start as a new person in Christ—as long as the new marriage is to another believer (see 2 Corinthians 6:14).

The second concession God makes, found in Matthew 19:9, is sexual immorality or marital unfaithfulness. In this passage, Christ is speaking specifically about adultery (which also includes homosexual conduct). The men of Jesus' day were divorcing their wives for ridiculous reasons, like her hair was too long, she had morning breath, she was overweight, and so on. They were getting divorces left and right for illegitimate reasons. Jesus cuts to the quick: "I tell you that anyone who divorces his wife, except for sexual immorality, and marries another woman commits adultery."

I do not believe Jesus is saying or implying that a one-night stand is automatically a cause for divorce. The Bible certainly does not condone this kind of behavior, but I know many, many marriages that have survived a one-time affair and are flourishing today by the grace and mercy of God. But if there is a pattern of unfaithfulness, it is one of the biblical grounds for divorce.

The third concession God gives us is in the case of desertion by an unbeliever. We find the scriptural support for this concession in 1 Corinthians 7:15: "But if the unbeliever leaves, let it be so." A believing man or woman is not bound to their unbelieving spouse in such circumstances. God has called us to live in peace. If a believer is married to an unbeliever, he or she is to live out their faith in a quiet, reverent, and holy manner. But if the unbeliever deserts the believer, the believer is free to remarry.

I believe a good argument can also be made that this particular concession applies to situations of sexual or physical abuse against a spouse or children. In a sense, the abusing spouse (whether a professing Christian or not) has spiritually deserted their family by endangering them with a pattern of deviant behavior that is both illegal and immoral. I would even question whether such a person could truly be a believer in Christ, if they indeed profess to be one. While abuse or other ongoing criminal activity is not given as an explicit reason for divorce, it seems to be implicit within this broader concession of desertion.

NOW WHAT?

One night, a close friend of comedian and satirist W.C. Fields walked into his dressing room to find W.C. reading the Bible. Now, you must understand something about W.C. Fields if you are not familiar with him. He was known to be a wild man: a womanizer, a drunk, and a poison-tongued performer. In short, he was immoral. Here, though, was W.C. propped back in his chair in front of the makeup mirror, reading the Bible. As he saw Fields thumbing through the pages of Scripture, this friend was shocked. He said, "W.C., what has happened? Why are you of all people reading the Bible?" W.C. Fields responded in classic style in that one-of-a-kind voice, "I'm just looking for loopholes. Looking for loopholes."

Too many of us read the Bible and look for loopholes. "Oh, there is a way out. Great, I can divorce her. I can divorce him and go along the primrose path." There is no primrose path after divorce. Believe me, I've seen many shattered marriages, and the path leading from those broken relationships is always a rocky and difficult one. God always wants us to look for a way to work through the problem. He does not give us these concessions for divorce as an easy out but as a last resort.

> **Divorce is not the unpardonable sin. God can make something new and wonderful out of the pieces of a broken marriage and family.**

The sad fact is, many have made the decision to divorce for one reason or another. You may be one of those people. And the question on your mind is, *Now what? Where do I go from here?* Let me encourage you that divorce is not the unpardonable sin. God can make something new and wonderful out of the pieces of a broken marriage and family. You can still achieve God's ideal for marriage the second time around.

With that in mind, I want to spend the remainder of this chapter outlining some creative ways to achieve a harmonious mix in a "blended family." Starting over after divorce is usually not just about you and your new spouse, because children are often involved. We will address remarriage, therefore, from the perspective of both the adults and the children involved in this new blended family situation.

CREATING A CREATIVE FAMILY BLEND

I want to share with you how you can have harmony in your new family. I want to share with you how you can experience unity and harmony in this recreated family band. To do this, I will use musical metaphors to illustrate the harmony you can achieve in a blended family. Paul encourages believers in Philippians 4:2, "Live in harmony in the Lord" (NASB). This applies to single adults. It applies to those who are married within a nuclear family. It also applies to the single parent family and the blended family. We are to live in harmony in the Lord.

In other words, God loves you and me so much that He cannot stand the thought of His people experiencing dissonance in their lives as a result of sin. His desire is for us to live in harmony with Him. He doesn't promise us an easy life by any means, but He does promise to be our God who will protect and love us unconditionally. "Well, how do I get that, Ed? I am remarried in a blended family. I am a single parent and dealing with all this mess. How do I experience harmony?"

AUDITION THE PLAYERS

Let's start with the basics. The first thing you have to do if you are considering remarriage and doing the blended family gig is audition the prospective musicians. If you talk to any good music director, he spends a good amount of time doing something called audition work. If a director or conductor just picked people at random to be a part of a band or choir, he would end up in chaos. The audience would say, "Oh, they have the worst music in the world. It doesn't make sense. It sounds like everyone is just doing his or her own thing. There's no mixing or blending."

It takes time to audition, to interview, and to determine how the individual parts of the band come together. If you are considering remarriage and taking on the blended family gig, you had better take time to interview all the prospective band members prior to marriage. Sit down with them, get to know them, and see how they mesh, because that's the time to discover how they will come together. Don't wait until after you are married to audition the prospective players.

Research and experience tell us that it takes two years emotionally to get over the death of a spouse or the trauma of divorce. Make sure you date your future mate long enough for everyone involved—the man, the woman, and the children—to get to a point where they are able to act naturally around each other.

We can all fool people; we are pros at doing that. We put on that game-show-host smile so others will think we never have a bad day. We work hard at giving the impression that everything is always perfect and that we are ready to tackle the world. All the while, though, we are hiding our true emotions inside. It takes time to see others for whom they truly are, so give everyone involved the time they need to feel comfortable enough around each other to behave naturally. You need time to discern why your divorce took place and the point of why your future spouse got their divorce. You need time to heal yourself spiritually and recalibrate anything in your life that is impeding your relationship with Christ. Can you handle the fact that your kids will potentially have multiple sets of parents? Will all the complex relationships mesh together?

We serve a God of second, third, and fourth chances. His grace keeps going and going and going. Just because you have been divorced, it is not the end of the world. You don't have to fly coach, spiritually speaking, as if you have to hide behind the curtain for the rest of your life, just because you have been divorced. Yes, you can still fly first class. God might lead you into the blended family unit or a remarriage situation just so you can have a second chance to achieve His ideal. You must take the time to get to know and understand the dynamics of everyone involved before taking the leap into a blended family situation.

REHEARSE, DON'T REPEAT

Musicians rehearse over and over again to keep from repeating past mistakes and to engrain positive patterns for the future. Hopefully and prayerfully, you come to the marital table during a second marriage with more maturity and with the experience of learning from past mistakes.

Something I have seen, though, is so many young people who come from divorced homes lean toward getting divorced in their own lives. If you have parents who have been divorced, you are more likely to get a divorce. Why in the world is this a trend? Why is this happening in such overwhelming numbers?

Here is one major reason why I believe this trend exists: parents who get divorced are not teaching their children to learn from their mistakes. If you are in this situation, take the time, energy, and effort to rehearse with your children where you went wrong and what you should have done differently. Take them aside and

say, "This is where Daddy messed up. This is where Mommy messed up. Divorce is not the best way to do it. I was wrong in this area, and this is what I should have done and what you should do in a relationship." Break the cycle, learn from your mistakes, and help your children learn from them as well. After explaining where you went wrong, begin modeling the godly way to structure a family—a family that is centered upon God and His Word.

FOCUS ON THE RIGHT SCORE

Also, if you are thinking about a remarriage that will create a blended family, take your eyes off the musical score of the nuclear family and focus on this new blended family score. Stop comparing your situation to the nuclear family of one man and one woman, together forever, with 2.3 kids. That is not the blended family. The blended family is a whole different scene, with multiple family situations happening at the same time. And if you're not careful, it has the potential to be a breeding ground for jealousy, envy, complications, mistakes, and hurt feelings.

> If you are thinking about a remarriage that will create a blended family, take your eyes off the musical score of the nuclear family and focus on this new blended family score.

You can be obedient to Philippians 4:2—living "in harmony in the Lord"—even in the blended family. But you are going to have to spend more time in the studio, more time working, and more time listening. If an opera singer, hip-hop artist, and a country music star stepped into a recording studio together, do you think they would achieve unity and harmony immediately? If they really worked at it, harmony could come eventually. But it doesn't just happen naturally. It takes time.

When I think about dissonant family situations in the Bible, I think about Jacob in Genesis 35. Jacob had four wives (two were sisters), twelve sons, and a meddling father-in-law. They all lived together in adjoining tents. Do you think they had a few problems? You bet they did. But out of that confusing family situation God brought the twelve tribes of Israel (through Jacob's sons).

You don't have to go to the movies or binge watch Netflix to see exciting stuff. Just read the Bible. Intrigue, espionage, murder, jealousy, envy, and strife—it's all in there. And the great thing is that we can learn from the mistakes of biblical characters so we don't have to make them ourselves. That is one of the reasons I love the Bible. God doesn't try to cover up the mistakes of His people or rationalize them away. He just lays it all on the line so we can benefit from the shortcomings and failures of other people of faith.

Eli is a character in the book of 1 Samuel who also dealt with problems related to family harmony. Eli's two sons, Hophni and Phinehas, were out of control. Eli was a priest, and his sons were stereotypical preacher's kids. I mean, these guys were over the edge. First Samuel 3:13 reveals that Eli failed in disciplining his own sons: "His sons made themselves vile, and he did not restrain them" (NKJV). But God gave Eli a second chance by giving him Samuel to raise.

Samuel was the son of Elkanah and Hannah, who left him in Eli's charge to be brought up in the temple as a man of God. It is evident that Eli did a much better job when he had a second chance. Samuel turned out to be one of Israel's greatest judges and prophets. Eli turned his past mistakes into future successes by learning from his failure and doing it God's way the second time around. You, too, can win the second time around if you keep your eyes on what God has called you to do. Stop focusing on the nuclear family or others' expectations for your life. Trust God to build a family that fears Him and a home where His love is found through every relationship.

BE SENSITIVE TO STYLE

Once you hear, "I now pronounce you husband and wife" and you are involved in the blended family, there is something else you don't want to miss. Be sensitive to the fact that each of the musicians has a different style. I am referring specifically to the children in the blended family.

You might not believe this, but remarriage is more difficult and taxing on children than divorce. They are going to go through more trauma during remarriage than during the divorce. "Why?" you ask. "That doesn't make sense." Remarriage is more difficult because when you get remarried, it ends the thought in the child's mind that reconciliation is still possible for their mom and dad. Also, they have to accept the new family unit with its new authority structure.

Another major issue for children, especially teenagers, is the invasion of their space. Suddenly, they have to share their stuff, maybe even their room, with new "family members" who might as well be strangers. Some of that discomfort can be alleviated by allowing sufficient time for both spouses and children to adjust to the new family prior to establishing a combined household. But it is still going to be a major adjustment.

Remember that within every family, especially the blended family, everyone needs their own stuff. If I were speaking, I would ask you to make eye contact and listen carefully. You need to be sure to give children their own territory, because from the child's per-spective, these "aliens" have suddenly come in, invaded their already-defined territory, and are messing with their stuff. Mom and Dad, make sure every person has some space, even if it is a little corner, just for them and their personal things. The same is true for creating defined personal space for the kids that are moving into the home as well.

The number one reason that the divorce rate is higher the second time around is the unique child rearing challenges of the blended family. I encourage you to take your children and your new spouse's children and audition them for the express purpose of getting to know them and becoming sensitive to their styles. If you will do this ahead of time, you will help them mesh more successfully into the new family system.

It is tempting to get so involved in the newly established marriage relationship that you tune out the changing needs of the children involved. Don't let that happen. Take the necessary time to understand and be sensitive to each child's unique style, before and after the new marriage begins.

> **Take the necessary time to understand and be sensitive to each child's unique style, before and after the new marriage begins.**

Recently, I pulled up to a busy intersection in the Dallas-Fort Worth area, and I heard (and *felt*) massive bass coming from the car behind me. I glanced back and saw this guy singing along like nobody's business to a song. People around him in the other cars were looking at him and laughing. The guy was totally oblivious, though. He was so into his style that it was like the rest of the world was not even there.

I see parents in a blended family doing the same thing. They have this love that is so fresh, so dynamic, and so all-encompassing with their new spouse that these two love birds forget about how it is affecting the kids involved on both sides. Meanwhile, the kids are thinking, *This blended family thing is the worst.* The new family is not just about Mom (or stepmom) and Dad (or stepdad). This is an all-for-one and one-for-all deal. It's about everyone involved. Are you sensitive to the styles of your children?

IT'S TIME FOR A NEW SONG

If you are going to have harmony and unity instead of dissonance, you will need to learn how to sing a new song. In Psalm 33:3, David writes, "Sing to him a new song." I am sure the first time David pulled out the harp and started strumming a new song, people probably thought, *Oh my, he is not singing traditional hymns anymore; the guy has gone contemporary. Who is this long-haired shepherd boy singing these rock songs? What has gotten into these Hebrew kids?* Well, David was singing a new song. Just like David, the blended family has to learn to sing a new song.

Do you know what tears families apart? Do you know what tears apart single parent families or blended families? It's when we get stuck and keep playing the same old song on repeat in our hearts and minds. Do you remember leisure suits and 8-track tapes? Be honest. I must confess that I had a lime green leisure suit, and it didn't have lapels—a serious fashion emergency. (If you don't know what that is, google it and enjoy a laugh.) I thought this leisure suit, unlike some that had giant lapels that looked like elephant ears, was the greatest thing in the world. I also had an 8-track tape player, and my favorite tape was "The Best of the Bee Gees." Talk about retro. Maybe when you go retro you think of playing songs from cassette tapes or CDs? For the even younger of us, maybe the first-generation iPod is going retro.

So many blended and single parent families make the mistake of going retro by trying to live with an "old-song mentality" that discourages you constantly and leaves you feeling that like nothing will ever change. What am I talking about? I am talking about not letting go of the anger and resentment of the broken relationship. "Oh, my ex is such a jerk." We play the tape or CD of bitterness over and over repeatedly. It's replayed for the ex-spouse and their new spouse, and then the kids get to hear it a few hundred times. The bitterness escalates and spreads like a disease. And as the hurt person continues to attack their ex, he or she returns the favor by attacking back.

How do you break out of this "old-song mentality"? Take the cassette tape or CD and throw it away! Get ready to start streaming a new song for you, for your family, and for your future that can only be given to you through Christ. What is unique about this new song? It begins with realizing that God can stream a new song to you anytime, anywhere, no matter what you are facing, to completely transform the rhythm of your life. There are no limits to what God will do in your life when you are able to stop looking back at your past and instead lock eyes with the future before you and embrace God's new song.

Philippians 3:13–14 says, "Brothers and sisters, I do not consider myself yet to have taken hold of it. But one thing I do: Forgetting what is behind and straining toward what is ahead, I press on toward the goal to win the prize for which God has called me heavenward in Christ Jesus."

What a powerful verse! This is one of my life verses. In fact, I preached from this passage the first Sunday I ever spoke at Fellowship Church. The apostle Paul was advising his friends in Philippi to forget the past and move forward. If there's anything in the past that keeps you from progress, you had better forget it.

I am glad we serve a God who tells me and you to forget what lies behind. Instead, He says, "Reach forward to what lies ahead." Isn't that great? It is time to live by that new song that Jesus has for you. Confess your sins, deal with them, work through the grief, join a local church, and move ahead one day at a time. Find someone at church who has gone through what you are going through and allow them to encourage you. God has a new agenda, a new course, a new avenue, a new highway for the blended family. God can give you the power to put the past behind you and press on.

CREATE HARMONY

I'm not a great singer, but I had the opportunity to be involved in a musical performance many years ago at my father's church in Houston, Texas. The music director of this church walked up to me one day and said, "Ed, I'm doing a musical and putting together a barbershop quartet. Since you have a really low voice, I wondered if you would like to sing the bass part. Would you consider it, Ed?"

I replied, "Well, no, I have never done that before. I don't know the first thing about singing in a barbershop quartet." He kept after me until I finally relented, "Okay, I will try out for it. I'll do the audition."

This is what my audition consisted of. The music director said, "Okay, Ed, find the lowest note that you can possibly produce and hold it there for about ten seconds." I did exactly that. I sang (or rumbled) the lowest note I could and held it for several seconds. And then he said, "That's it, Ed. You've got it." I said "What?" He said, "That's it! That's all we need." The day of the big event came at the Music Hall in downtown Houston, and I was the bass singer in the barbershop quartet. When the music director nodded to me, I would just let out that one note until he cut me off. People came up to me afterwards and said, "Oh, what a beautiful voice. That was unbelievable. You sure know how to create that harmony, Ed."

I couldn't help but laugh at their applause and compliments, because I knew how pathetic I sounded without the talent of the three other men and the guidance of the music director. Creating that kind of harmony was definitely a group effort. And that is what we are talking about with the blended family—creating harmony together. How do you harmonize as a family? Too many of us are relationally tone deaf, or we are operating without musical direction. We don't know how to harmonize with each other.

In seminary I was required to take a music class where I learned the basics of conducting. If you are really going to do the blended family gig, you must establish harmony in the home by becoming co-conductors with your spouse. You need to join hands and learn how to conduct your blended family together. If you don't, Mom will be reading one piece of music, and Dad will be reading another piece of music. That's how you spell dissonance. You must come together with one musical sheet in front of you as your guide.

When you direct, make sure you don't try to improvise and defect from the sheet of music from which you have both agreed to conduct. That is an easy temptation to fall into in the blended family. What often happens is that you initially agree with your spouse to become co-conductors in discipline, in responsibilities, and in rules. But as time goes by and the rubber hits the road, you begin to cut a little more slack with your biological children than with your stepchildren. You begin to get a little more sensitive and defensive about their needs, and you start to defect from the musical piece you've all agreed to play.

It is human nature to be more protective of your biological children and to want to have more freedom with them. Make sure, though, that you sit down with your spouse and set forth in writing what every person's responsibility will be in the blended family. Also, define how those various responsibilities will mesh with or bleed over into the ex-spouse's family unit. You must set those principles, put them down, and direct together.

This includes working with your ex-spouse in the other household and having some common ground on which you can both stand for the sake of the children. The children must feel, especially in a joint-custody situation, that they are vital members of both households. This can only happen when everyone works together from the same page.

SINGLE PARENTS

I want to push the pause button and address a specific issue facing single parents that can spill over into the blended family when they choose to remarry. We have so many single parents in society today, and I think they have one of the most difficult and underappreciated roles. I have seen so many wonderful things happen over the years as God has worked through and touched single parents, giving them power and ability well beyond their years and capacity. I want to share with you several things you need to understand regarding this single parent game.

When a divorce occurs, the wife usually experiences a significant cut in personal income. Because the wife is the custodial parent in most cases, her earning potential goes down as she attempts to juggle her work responsibilities with the increased demands of single parenting. The man, on the other hand, experiences a substantial increase in his personal income, because he is now able to devote most of his time to work.

Throughout this whole scenario, single moms are especially susceptible to feelings of guilt. They feel guilty for putting their children through the divorce, for being spread too thin between the home and career fronts, and for not being able to do more financially for their kids. Single moms, you can feel so guilty and so bitter that you end up trying to get rid of the guilt by becoming overly permissive with your children. Watch out for this tendency. You will allow your children to do anything, because you reason, *Well, if I am a nice mom, then I can make up for these other problems caused by my divorce.* Your children suddenly begin to run over you, and you treat them like one of your peers. And the authority base is gone.

Let's briefly shift gears to single dads. While both parties feel guilty in a divorce, single dads usually feel this guilt because you may not be as involved with your kids on a day-to-day basis as your ex-wife. This guilt leads you to become the purchasing parent. On weekend visits, there's entertainment, excitement, and adventure with Dad. You ease the guilt by getting into this "Do-It-All-With-Dad" mentality. Again, the authority base disappears, and your kids tumble into a free fall of deteriorating structure and discipline. I understand that the roles I just described can easily flip between each parent depending on the season or situation, but Lisa and I have generally found that these are the parenting temptations for which you need to be on the lookout.

We used to live a few houses down from a single mom and her three children, and even a casual observer on our street would notice a recurring event in that household. Once a week, this woman's ex-husband would turn down the street in his black SUV, pull up to the house, and walk to the door. A few minutes later, he would come out with the kids and proceed to take them to his home for the weekend. One week, as he turned the corner, I noticed that in the back of his truck he had brought with him an enormous box from

Toys R Us. He drove up to the house as usual and walked to the door. Out came his excited children, exclaiming, "Oh, Daddy's got a new toy! See you, Mom."

Single parents, I am talking to both moms and dads right now: please make sure you deal with the guilt between you and God and between you and your ex-spouse so that the effects of that guilt don't spill out onto your children. If you are going to mess up, mess up on the side of being too strict, rather than having a permissive mentality that says, "Well, kids, if it feels good, do it. You can do whatever you want and have whatever you want. I just want to make you happy."

THE BLENDED FAMILY

Let's release the pause button now and fast forward to the blended family. What often happens when a single mom or a single dad remarries and enters a blended family situation is that this permissive parenting style continues. That is why in many circumstances children run the show in the blended family. They ran the show when Mom and Dad were single, so they think the same rules apply in the blended family. Only this time, the stakes are even higher. You must establish that authority before you remarry so you can maintain that authority as co-directors in the blended family. Talk to any member of a band or orchestra, and they will tell you that someone has to call the shots. Mom and Dad must present a unified front as co-conductors.

Another aspect to being a good director and establishing harmony in the home is respecting the routines of the new family system. Establish your own routines as a blended family but also respect the routines of the other family, especially during the holiday shuffle. As the kids move from home to home, be extra sensitive to both your children's needs and those of the other family involved. Step up to the relational plate and do as much as you can to enhance your child's relationship with your ex-spouse.

If you have a problem with your ex-spouse, don't tell your child, "Well, your dad is just a jerk. That's why we got a divorce." If you have a problem with your ex-spouse, if they truly are being a jerk, talk to them about it. Don't use your child as a go-between or as relational ammunition. By being a parent and a role model, even in the midst of your toughest relational challenges, you can give your children the tools they need to establish lasting relationships later in life.

We have addressed several key issues related to divorce and remarriage in this chapter. We have looked at God's ideal for marriage and some biblical concessions for divorce. Following that, we discussed the opportunity for a second chance to achieve that marital ideal in the blended family. As you follow the principles related to creating a creative family blend—auditioning the players, rehearsing not repeating, focusing on the right score, being sensitive to style, replacing your old songs with a new song, and becoming co-conductors—you can experience the harmony of everyone pulling together in this new family band. Always remember that every family member is made stronger when the family is involved in a local church. All of this is the kind of music God loves to hear.

The Basics of *Creative* Harmony

- Remember, God's model is one man and one woman together in marriage, and He has provided the resources (through the Holy Spirit) to carry you through rocky times.

- Receive the reconciliation of God's grace and power so you can overcome the obstacles of divorce. God does hate divorce, but He can reconcile all things to give you another opportunity to do marriage His way.

- Take time (2–3 years) to heal after a divorce before you decide to remarry.

- Let God heal you so you can focus on the future rather than the past.

- Single parents should maintain control of their children despite the pressures to treat their children as if they were peers.

CHAPTER 8

Marital FAQS

ANSWERS TO SOME FREQUENTLY ASKED QUESTIONS ABOUT MARRIAGE

8

OVER THE LAST several chapters we have addressed issues like the Marital Work Ethic, creative communication, conflict resolution, and even the popular yet often avoided subject of sex. We also addressed the very important subjects of money and marriage and the challenge of keeping your family spouse-centric rather than kid-centric. And in the previous chapter, we tackled the difficult issues of divorce and remarriage.

In this chapter, Lisa and I will answer some frequently asked questions (FAQs) regarding marriage. These questions were solicited from people at our church during a series on marriage, and we believe they represent problems and issues for nearly every marital relationship.

Before we examine these questions, let me say something that you need to understand. Lisa and I are not experts on marriage. But we do enjoy a great marriage, and the reason we do is because we have built our lives on the principles found in God's Word. We have done this individually, and we have done it together as a couple.

I know some who will read this book are single adults. The church is full of single adults who are planning for, dreaming of, and thinking about marriage. On any given Sunday, a great percentage of those who attend Fellowship Church are single. We want to address some of the questions that singles have about marriage.

All married couples experience varying degrees of difficulty at different times in their marriage. We will do our best to address some of the issues you are dealing with right now in this final chapter.

It is a pipe dream for Lisa and me to think we can understand and feel exactly what you are feeling. We can, on the other hand, hit on these common marital issues and direct you to the material and counselors out there who can help make your marriage a creative and lasting one.

Q: The first chapter talked about the value of the marriage vows. If I have already said these vows, or will in the future, how do I know for sure the other person is the right one?

ED: Well, hopefully you know that your fiancée is the right one prior to standing before a pastor, God, and some friends for the event! What I share with singles in counseling situations comes from both the Bible and from life experiences. I have written a book entitled *Rating Your Dating While Waiting for Mating*, which breaks down a lot of what I teach. But let me give you the Cliff Notes of this book. If you are single and considering a specific someone as a possible life partner, I think there are several tests that you need to take him or her through.

The first test would be the spiritual test. You need to make sure that they know

> **When you are both operating from the same spiritual dynamic, it forms the foundation for conflict resolution.**

Christ personally. I am not talking about just lip service but an actual story about their life before Christ, what happened when they met the Lord, and what God has done since that important event.

When you are both operating from the same spiritual dynamic, it forms the foundation for conflict resolution. Marriage is about conflict in a real way. You have two self-centered sinners trying to do life God's way, so you need to be on the same page spiritually and also have knowledge of the ministry of reconciliation.

We need to try to understand the idea that God sent Christ to die on the cross for our sins, something we don't deserve, and that He rose again. If we have accepted that, we have been given the ability and motivation to want to make our issues right before God and before our spouse.

Speaking of the spiritual test, it also helps in raising children. Lisa and I raised four children. Child rearing is challenging, and I don't know where we would be without that common bond of Christ.

I would also use the character test. It is important to objectively measure the other person's character. Because Lisa and I dated for a long time, I was able to observe her in various situations. Honesty, responsibility, endurance, and other important qualities like these can only be seen over the long haul.

Another test would be the one of just kicking back, hanging out, and living life on the rugged plains of reality. You might call this the time test. If you are dating and contemplating marriage, I would advise dating at least 12 months. What this does is allow infatuation to fade like a good pair of jeans. It will help you discern the relationship through good times and bad. Time will also allow you expose the relationship to family and friends. We all know there's nothing quite as helpful as the counsel we receive from the people who know us best.

Q: Lisa, when did you know that Ed was the right one for you?

LISA: As Ed mentioned, we dated for six years. We met when we had just finished our freshman year of high school. We had dated just one year when Ed told me that we were going to get married. I told him that was great, but I wanted to grow up and be a flight attendant and fly all over the world. I told him he would have to wait until after that if he really wanted to get married.

By the time we were sophomores in college, I reminded him that he had once said we were going to get married. I told him I no longer had the desire to be a flight attendant and that we should get the show on the road.

During these six years, we had already answered those questions and passed those tests. Ed's integrity and character had been on full display through several challenging seasons. After all that time together, I just knew in my heart that a part of me would be empty without him. And I believed he felt the same way.

Q: The third chapter addressed the importance of communication between a husband and a wife. Ed, you are the pastor of a very large church and are very, very busy. Lisa, you serve at the church as well as take care of your husband, and you raised four children. How in the world do you two build time into your marriage for communication?

LISA: We are very busy, and I think most people these days are very busy. This is definitely one of the killers of good communication. I think many of us have forgotten the art of saying "no." We need to learn to let go of the good things in order to receive the best things in life.

Ed and I are very intentional about building time together on a daily and weekly basis in order to communicate. It doesn't just happen. There will always be a family member who needs us. There will always be people in our church who need us. So we are very intentional about it.

When we had little ones in the house, we structured time daily after the children were in bed for the night. The same is true for when our grandkids are with us now. I am a very structured person, and we are big on enforcing an established bedtime during school nights. Back in the day, our high-school-aged youth went to bed later, but they would be upstairs having their quiet time in the evenings so Ed and I could enjoy some adult time together. Another important element is what we did then and now with our extra-curricular activities (ECAs). We say no to a lot of these ECAs that can get in the way of our time together in the evenings.

Also, we went years with not having a television in our bedroom. A great thing happened when the TV in our bedroom broke early on in marriage. This "TV-free zone" created a better atmosphere for communication. If you have a TV in your bedroom, be very friendly with the "Off" button. That time together in silence will allow you to communicate. This communication can lead you to some great "other things" as well. Enough said.

And then there is our date night, which Ed addressed earlier in the book. We schedule one at least every other week, but we try to date every week. If the daily communication has been difficult, by Thursday night we know we will be together for an uninterrupted time.

Oftentimes on our dates, I have the calendar in hand so that we can go over our schedule for the next week. It may be humorous, but it may also be the only time we have to schedule things we want to do. If we don't schedule well in advance, time will be eaten away by other things.

ED: We must fight for that time. I would say that it has been the date night that has taken our marriage to the next level. You know, it's great to go out with other couples, but that concentrated time for just the two of us is crucial.

LISA: On occasion we go out with others, but we keep it balanced. There were times when I had meetings at the school and had to excuse myself for not attending. I used to wish I had some big excuse other than the fact that Ed and I were going on a date that night. But I finally got the courage to say that, and the other wives were falling all over themselves to tell me how great that was. This concept became something that many of my friends wanted to adopt for themselves.

Q: What do you think is the most important thing a spouse can communicate to his or her partner?

ED: I would say that self-esteem is right up there. Both the husband and the wife get much of their self-esteem and value from each other. Oftentimes, I have forgotten the importance of my words to Lisa. Maybe I have said a word of criticism to her. Maybe Lisa has done something incredible, and I have not really complimented her the way I should have. I am trying to improve my sensitivity in this area because I haven't been as consistent as I should be.

I think of our church. I have the opportunity to speak before a lot of people several times each weekend. I certainly appreciate it when people come up to tell me they liked the message. But there is nothing like having Lisa turn to me on the way home and say, "Honey, I really appreciated that message. It really blessed my heart." There is nothing like hearing that from my wife. The self-esteem thing is big. Don't forget the little things either. Things like honoring her with positive body language and big hugs are also very meaningful.

LISA: I feel it is important for Ed to show me that I am valuable, and for me to show him that he is valuable. We do that by being intentional about our communication and having that time alone together.

We must be careful about the things we do that could possibly devalue our spouse, like mentioning them in a negative light in public conversation, setting up a date night and not showing up, or spending time on the phone instead of being alone with them. You also must be careful in how you convey messages to your spouse through both your tone of voice and your words. When Ed and I speak words of value to each other, we gain more confidence in one another and in our marriage.

Q: Moving from communication to conflict resolution, how do you two handle financial stress in your marriage?

ED: Many couples have financial stress and pressure. Maybe one spouse seems like they have an Amazon package delivered daily, and the other one is more conservative. This is often the case in marriage. Or maybe both are drowning in a sea of debt. There is no pressure like financial pressure on the marriage relationship.

I challenge husbands and wives to have a biblical view of money. What Lisa and I have tried to do over the years of our marriage is acknowledge that everything we have comes from God. That is a no-brainer for us.

Usually, we sit down at the beginning of the year and go over our budget for the coming twelve months. We live pretty much by the 10-10-80 principle. We give at least 10 percent to the church. We have given much more than that at times, but that is our baseline. Then we try to save at least 10 percent, and we live on the remaining 80 percent. When we are talking and praying about the budget, these give us some basic guidelines.

I think some couples make serious mistakes when one spouse has an account that the other doesn't know about—a little 007-style action. I think there should be full disclosure, and you need to talk about major purchases together before you make them. Lisa and I even defined in advance what a major purchase is and agreed to only proceed together.

LISA: Usually, we talk about the goals we have for the year. I like to talk about furniture, and Ed usually likes to discuss his next fishing trip. We talk about our family vacation, and we put in money for emergencies. We don't go into that conversation selfishly but think about one another and the whole family picture. With the remaining 80 percent, after giving and saving, it is about how we can use wisely what God has blessed us with to pay our bills, to eat, and to enjoy ourselves.

> **With the remaining eighty percent, after giving and saving, it is about how we can use wisely what God has blessed us with to pay our bills, to eat, and to enjoy ourselves.**

Q: You talked about full disclosure regarding finances. What is your view on pre-nuptial agreements that people use to negotiate a marriage?

ED: If someone is thinking about a pre-nuptial agreement, we would challenge them to seriously consider the reasons why they feel it is needed. Are they unsure of the other person? Is there an element of distrust or uncertainty about that person or about whether the marriage will last? If that's the case, they need to rethink the marriage or begin some pre-marital counseling to work through those issues. Generally speaking, we don't like these types of agreements in marriage, because we don't think you should go into marriage with a question mark. You should go into marriage with an exclamation point.

LISA: Now, understand that we had less than $1,800 to our name when we got married.

ED: Well, that's true! Even so, that is still what we'd advise. You don't want to go into marriage being unsure. Trust is foundational to any great marriage.

Q: How do you deal with the controversial concept of submission in your family?

ED: That whole issue in the Bible has been misconstrued and taken out of context. Here is what the Bible says: the husband has the spiritual responsibility in the relationship. He is the leader. It doesn't mean that he is on a pedestal and the wife is below him.

We play on a level playing field before God. However, according to the Bible, the husband is to love his bride like Jesus loved the Church. How much did He love the Church? He laid down His life for the Church. Christ took the initiative and never stops working for the Church. Even though we don't deserve to be loved, He loves us.

If I love Lisa with a self-sacrificing love, she is free and will experience great freedom to be submissive. She is able to love me yet live her life like she wants it to be done.

There are many times when we have big decisions. I think that maybe we should go a certain way, but Lisa will point out other factors that she thinks should be included in the decision. She can and often does bring up things that cause me to change my mind. But I know at the end of the day, as far as God's chain of command goes, the final decision rests on the shoulders of the husband, and I take that responsibility very seriously.

LISA: I have never had a problem with the term "submission." I have had a problem submitting! When I think of this issue, I cannot help thinking of something that happened early in our marriage.

We wanted to go visit my family in South Carolina for Thanksgiving, but we only had a short amount of time. Both of us were in school, and he was also working. Ed wanted to fly, but I told him that we could not afford it and that we would have to drive. We went back and forth on this issue.

We had just gotten our first credit card, which came with a $350 limit. The tickets were going to be $175 each. I told Ed that if we bought them, we would be making a mistake. We didn't need to have debt, and I thought that we should drive instead. (Now, I did not mention that there was a piece of furniture I wanted to bring back with us. I only used the financial consequences to influence Ed's thinking.)

One night, Ed sat up in bed and announced, "We are flying." He got out of bed and proceeded to make the flight arrangements in the middle of the night. I was really upset. And I must confess that on this occasion, I did not follow the biblical principle of resolving my anger before I went to bed. The next day I was still fuming. Even though I was submitting on the outside, I was still very upset about it on the inside. When we got to the airport, the flight was overbooked. The gentleman at the counter said that we could have free seats on a later flight if we gave up our tickets. He also gave us money for a cab, movies, and dinner.

When we eventually flew to South Carolina, we made the entire trip without spending a dime. God taught me that submission is a really good thing to practice! I realize this may be kind of an extreme example, and I'm not promising that you'll fly free if you submit to your husband. But I believe God was teaching me an important lesson about having a submissive attitude through that experience.

ED: It is interesting that the word *husband* in Latin is made up of two words: "house" and "band." We are to be the band that keeps the marriage and the household together.

Let's say that in a particular situation, your wife is 99.9 percent wrong, and you are 0.1 percent wrong. Even then, husbands are to be the ones to initiate the reconciliation. That is the spiritual responsibility of the husband. Even on the days when she may be hard to love, you are to love your wife like Christ loved the Church. And believe me, if you are doing that, the other pieces will take care of themselves.

LISA: It is also something that brings order to a household. Ed mentioned the chain of command. There are times when I will share my opinions with him; sometimes he takes them, and other times he goes with his initial decision. He is not always right, but it is nothing that is beyond repair. We both use each decision and each circumstance as a learning lesson and recognize that this process of submission and self-sacrificing love is the order of our household.

ED: There are many other areas in which Lisa leads for our family. For example, we were talking about finances. She is the one who pays the bills. In our relationship, she is the one who happens to have a better gift in this area. However, I am still engaged in our finances, and I don't allow Lisa to carry the weight of responsibility solely on her alone.

Q: How do you deal with the issue of in-laws in the marriage?

LISA: I do not have the typical mother-in-law situation. Ed and I dated for six years. There are three boys in his family, and I was the only girl on the scene for a very long time. And to be honest with you, Ed's mother spoiled me rotten. She and I had a great relationship from the very beginning. When she used to come and visit, it was a lot of fun for me to have her here.

However, in the early days of our marriage, my family lived in South Carolina, and we lived in Houston, very close to Ed's family. I had done that leave and cleave part that the Bible talks about in Genesis 2. I left my family, and I was holding very tightly to the relationship I had with my new husband.

Ed, on the other hand, was still very close to his family. He continued to do things just about the same way he had always done things. If I expected him home for dinner, he might be over there shooting baskets with his brothers. When I would find him, I would ask what he was doing, and he would say that he was "home"—but not our home! So it was kind of tough in those early days.

ED: I had a tougher time cutting the cord than she did. Also, living in Houston and working at the same church where my father was (and still is) the pastor was great, but it was also tough for Lisa and me. It was hard to figure out where the father began and the boss ended. I think one of the greatest things for our marriage was when we moved to the Dallas-Fort Worth area.

LISA: Now, the in-laws for Ed and for me are very important. Our parents are huge. When we first relocated to Dallas and went to buy our house, we strongly valued the opinion of our parents. We listened to some of their advice, but we still had plenty of decisions to tough out on our own.

ED: It's funny; neither set of parents liked the choice we made in that first home in Dallas. They thought it was too old and that we would have to pay too much for repairs.

LISA: We valued their opinion. However, our decision was based on our prayer time together and our communication with each other. One of the unhealthiest reactions you can have is running to Mama or Papa rather than looking to your spouse.

Q: How would you advise people to deal with the in-laws when they pressure their adult children to spend the holidays with them?

LISA: For us, holidays are kind of tough. For Easter, we are here for our church services. For Christmas, it is the same situation. We decided early on to spend the holidays in a way that is best for our family.

So we do everything in our home and invite the grandparents to come see us. That worked out great for us when our kids were in the home. There were times when we spent Christmas at grandparents' homes during a portion of the holiday or at Thanksgiving, but for the most part, it is our deal. We definitely want our children's grandparents to be a big part of their lives, but we had to choose what was best for our family. As you look at the stages and ages of your kids and consider other factors that may be impacting your family, you get to choose what works best for you.

ED: We try to spend the big holidays (Christmas being the biggest) at home. And then after Christmas, if we want to go see the extended family, we'll do that.

Q: We know that an alarming number of marriages end in divorce. What would you have to say about divorce, especially as it relates to those in the church who have gone through or are considering a divorce?

ED: Well, divorce is neither the unpardonable nor the unforgivable sin. Let me say that first of all. We serve a God of second chances. I know many people who have gone through the devastation of divorce, and there is a light at the end of the tunnel.

God's ideal is for one man and one woman to get married and stay married until they die. However, the Bible does mention three grounds for divorce, which I've already outlined in the previous chapter. The first would be when a divorce occurs prior to belief in Christ; the second, adultery; and the third, desertion. Even so, these are given as a last resort after we have done everything possible to save the marriage.

These biblical grounds for divorce have various nuances. And if you want to delve more into that, there are some great Christian books you can read for more detailed information on this issue. I would also encourage you to ask your church or pastor for a referral to a good, biblically-based Christian counselor who can help clarify this issue.

My heart goes out to divorced men and women. I want to minister to their needs. For the most part, no matter how high the price, it is important to try to make the marriage work since the price of divorce is higher. I can think of maybe nine or ten cases over the years where that wouldn't have been true, but there are thousands of others where the marriage could have been salvaged.

> **For the most part, no matter how high the price, it is important to try to make the marriage work since the price of divorce is higher.**

LISA: And those several he is mentioning are cases where one spouse was very abusive, was in prison for long standing drug abuse, or some other extreme situation.

ED: But I would say to those who are divorced that you can use your experiences, what you learned from the first marriage, and apply that in your second marriage. You can do the next marriage God's way.

That is why we wrote this book and why we have resources available at our church, as well as numerous classes and seminars about marriage. So get involved in your church, find the help you need, and do it God's way.

LISA: An important thing to consider before heading to divorce is the sacrifice God made for all of us. If you are in a situation where things are very rocky and divorce looks imminent, think about the price God paid when our sin separated us from Him, and our relationship with Him was severed. God paid the ultimate price through His Son, Jesus Christ, to reconcile us. He sent His only Son to die on the cross so that we could be totally restored.

When you consider what God did for our relationship with Him, why wouldn't we work harder to give our marriage another chance?

Whether you were married on a hillside in Maui or a stained-glass church in the city, when you said, "I do," it was a covenant before God. And God does not take lightly the breaking of the covenant.

We live in a very disposable, quick-fix society, and oftentimes, that tends to be the pull. But I pray that you will consider what God has done for you and decide to work harder to give the relationship every opportunity. Today is a new day. It can be a new day in your relationship.

ED: We know that a frightening number of divorces occur in the earliest years of marriage. What that tells me is that during the early years of adjustment, conflict was not handled properly. When you don't crash through those quitting points that we all face, you end up deciding to bail out.

What happens is that you find yourself in a repetitive cycle where the same kind of junk ends up surfacing in the next marriage and the next marriage and the next marriage.

Q: Looking back at your marriage, what was one of the most stressful times you had to navigate through and what did you learn from it?

ED: I would say the first couple of years were tough, and going from two children to four children when the twins were born was a big adjustment. At that time, we were building our new church complex in Grapevine, Texas, and we were still holding four services a weekend in rented facilities. That was a taxing time to say the least. We had to be extremely creative in how we maintained a healthy rhythm for our marriage and family. We needed to quickly learn how to communicate more effectively and pause some unhelpful habits on how we handled conflict.

LISA: Referring to the time when our twins were born, we experienced mounting pressure from all fronts. When this kind of pressure is going on, expect it to carry over to your marital relationship, too. You must do things to safeguard your relationship.

One of the biggest problems we faced was not fighting fair. When arguments came up and conflict arose, we did not use those biblical boundaries that keep the conflict in a positive light.

It sounds a little strange, but conflict can be a very positive thing for your relationship. Back then, though, we tended to name call and compare. Ed is a great imitator, and he would throw that in the mix. I have a strong capacity to get historical with him, remembering every past failure he has committed in our marriage. Needless to say, we weren't exactly fighting fairly!

These conflicts were negative, and they didn't do anything to elevate our relationship. If anything, they tore both of our self-esteems down. Conflict can be beneficial if you fight fairly and come to a resolution. Once this happens, your relationship is taken to a higher level.

Also, Ed and I believe that some arguing needs to be done in front of the children. Now, that might sound strange, but if done properly, you are modeling conflict resolution for your children.

Our children did see us disagree from time to time. We did not get into heated battles in front of them, but they do know that we hold varying opinions on certain things. We still model it for our kids today. They see Ed's leadership role and how he listens to my opinions. They also see how forgiveness works in a relationship.

If you argue in front of your children but do not resolve it in front of them, then we would consider that unhealthy. But if you show forgiveness and resolution, you are modeling for them how to handle issues on the playground and how to handle tense times with their friends. Most importantly, you are showing them how to handle conflict in their future marriage relationship.

Q: In the chapter on sex builders and sex busters, you talked about the husband and wife fulfilling each other's sexual needs. How often should a couple have sex?

ED: I think about 1 Corinthians 7, where it says that we should not deprive one another except when we mutually agree for a time of prayer. We try to live that out. I think couples that try to hit some national average or whatever are missing the point.

We are to satisfy each other creatively, intentionally, strategically, and lovingly. So when one is in the mood and one is not (and that is often the norm), the one with the lesser desire should fulfill his or her duty to the spouse in an enthusiastic way.

Not just "Wait, you mean *again* tonight?" Giving of ourselves sexually is part of our discipleship. Some day we will be held accountable before God on how we served our spouse sexually.

When one partner wants to say "no" for whatever reason, it should be no with an appointment. Lisa and I wrote on this subject in more detail in our book *The Sexperiement*. We believe it will help you as you seek to meet your spouse's needs and grow in your intimacy together.

Q: How do you keep the fires of intimacy burning in marriage?
LISA: Well, we really work hard at understanding, knowing, and satisfying the other's needs. When you are talking about intimacy in marriage, there are certain physical needs that you need to discuss. But we have found that romance is a huge part of it.

What happens in the bedroom does not start there. It is a whole package deal, which includes valuing one another, what we say to one another, and our date night. We have common interests, and we enjoy our relationship.

Ed and I have a lot of fun together. I think creativity definitely plays a huge role. We both love the excitement that comes from a new dining or entertainment adventure. The key is to mix it up. Don't always go to the same places. Try going your whole date night with just $20. Recreate the events of your dating relationship.

We laugh a lot together. We enjoy going places together. Sometimes it means I need to do some things for Ed that I wouldn't naturally do. Other times, Ed will compromise for my benefit. We enjoy animals, Vietnamese food, and movies. We are also both athletic and enjoy sports. I don't really get into fly-fishing, but he loves it. I can communicate how much I value Ed by watching fly-fishing shows with him or bringing a new video home regarding fly-fishing techniques.

Ed is not into the theater as much as I am, but sometimes we will go see a play or musical together. Going to antique stores is not his favorite thing to do, but I like it. So we do things like that for each other.

ED: We try to appreciate each other's interests, and that helps. I agree that creativity is huge. We do a lot of fun stuff together and are always trying new things.

When we have those common bonds and experiences together outside the bedroom and communicate very openly about likes and dislikes in the bedroom, it keeps the house hot.

Q: Ed, you talk often about the importance of the church in every Christ follower's life. How important has the church been in your marriage?

ED: Well, even if we were not in the ministry, we would still reap the marital benefits of being connected to a local church. The Christians in the New Testament were always *connected* to a local church. What I mean by connected is they came together corporately but also met in small groups.

Lisa and I have some friends in our church family that we just love. We share challenges and victories. We are after the same goal—to glorify Christ in our marriage. It is important to expose your relationship to others who have common values. That is why we talk on and on in our church about our small groups and connection classes.

If you are a couple or a single adult and you are not involved in a smaller gathering (small groups or classes in your church), you need to get involved in the lives of other believers. This is a time when you can learn from the Bible and discuss some issues that are applicable to whatever stage of life you are in. You also deepen your walk by getting to know other couples on a more intimate level. This will keep you accountable with couples who share your beliefs and goals.

I would definitely say that without the church, our marriage would only be a four out of ten, rather than the nine or ten it is today.

LISA: The church has taught us, through the study of Scripture, how to have a daily walk with the Lord individually. We do not have a set time in our home when we open the Bible and have devotions together. Ed studies all week, and he has his personal quiet time. I have my personal time of study early in the morning. Then, as a family, we often prayed openly and read Scripture before dinner when all our kids lived with us. But I would not say that nightly family devotions are the rule for us.

We were also very proactive about teaching our children by capitalizing on teachable moments. For instance, while carpooling one day, I noticed that a critical conversation was going on in the car regarding some students in their classes and various teachers. I shared with them what I had been reading in the

Bible regarding the power of words and the impact that negative words have on us. So the influence of the church and the Holy Spirit is a daily flow for us.

Of course, when we prayed with our children before they went to bed, we talked to them during this time about the issues they were dealing with.

The great thing about the church is that we can find others connected to Christ who share the same goals we have in our marriage and raise their children in a similar way. That is enormously helpful.

A FINAL THOUGHT FROM
ED AND LISA YOUNG

We have been in the ministry for many years, and we cannot stress enough to each person who is reading this book the importance of the local church in the life of your marriage.

We intentionally ended the book with this critical issue, because none of what we have talked about will be possible without the support of a local body of believers. The mutual encouragement, the service from and to others, the biblical accountability, and so many other aspects of the church are vitally important as you build and elevate your lives together.

And even more fundamental is the impact that the church will make on the lives of your children, now and forever.

If you don't take anything else away from this book, we urge you to find a church and get involved. We know it can be uncomfortable at first, but the effort is well worth the eternal rewards.

Certainly, if you live in the Dallas/Fort Worth area, Lisa and I welcome you to visit Fellowship Church in person or online. We'd love for you to discover God in a creative and dynamic environment, where you can learn in very practical ways more about what it means to be a Christ-follower and enjoy a creative and lasting marriage.

ABOUT ED AND LISA YOUNG

Ed and Lisa Young are the founding pastors of Fellowship Church, one of the most attended churches in North America over the past three decades. What started as a small group of families in the Dallas/Fort Worth area has grown to multiple locations including several prison campuses and a large online following.

As a best-selling author, Ed has written 15 books on the topics of leadership, Christian living, marriage, and parenting. Ed and Lisa have written several books together including *The Marriage Mirror, The Creative Marriage,* and the *New York Times* best-seller *Sexperiment: 7 Days to Lasting Intimacy with Your Spouse.*

Ed is also a frequent conference speaker noted for his creative communication style. He has a passion for making the complex simple and for seeing the local church thrive by resourcing church leaders through CreativePastors.com and the Creative Church Conference (C3).

Ed and Lisa have been married for more than forty years. They have four adult children and five grandchildren, and they live in the Dallas/Fort Worth area.

9 781950 113743